# MIND MAGIC: TECHNIQUES FOR TRANSFORMATION

## MARTA HIATT, PH.D

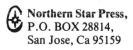 **Northern Star Press,**
P.O. BOX 28814,
San Jose, Ca 95159

Printed in the United States of America

Cover design and art work by Mary Ellen Guraro

Copies of this book may be ordered from:
    Northern Star Press,
    P.O. BOX 28814,
    San Jose, Ca 95159

Bulk Discount:
10-25 copies——10 percent
26-35 copies——20 percent
36-50 copies——30 percent
Over 50 copies—40 percent

California residents please add 7 percent sales tax
Shipping and Handling: Add $1.00 for any number of copies.
Price: $10.00 (In Canada: $11.00)

ISBN No: 0-9620929-0-8
Library of Congress Catalog Card Number: 88-65054

# DEDICATION

To those great souls, both here and hereafter
who have most inspired me, Edward L. Crump,
Katherine Calhoun, and Dr. Thurman Fleet of the
Concept-Therapy Institute, this book is lovingly dedicated.

By the same Author:
**Wisdom Teachings & Inspirational Quotations from the Concept-Therapy Philosophy.**
—Angel Press, 1972

## ACKNOWLEDGEMENTS

My great appreciation to my editor, Dot James, for her invaluable contribution, loving support, and many hours of hard work, improving and elucidating this book.

I am also grateful to all my students, from whom I have learned much over the years; and my clients who, through observing them coping with and resolving their problems, have taught me a great deal about the wonderous workings of the human mind, and how to live a successful life in this "best of all possible worlds."

Classes in the **PSYCHOLOGY OF SUCCESSFUL LIVING**
are conducted regularly in the San Francisco Bay Area
by Dr. Hiatt. Contact her at:
P.O. Box 28814,
San Jose, Ca 95159
or Telephone: (408) 287-5180


Classes in **CONCEPT-THERAPY** are conducted regularly
throughout the United States and Canada by the
Concept-Therapy Institute
25550 Boerne Stage Road,
San Antonio, Texas 78228.
(Please send for free brochures)

# CONTENTS

# CONTENTS

# LIST OF CHARTS

# A WORD TO THE READER

Although many books have been written on a single technique for improving one's life, this book presents a great variety of proven methods, while at the same time explaining *why* and *how* these life-transforming techniques work.

The book is divided into two parts. **PART I** is a study of the nature of consciousness, and how our minds work. To use the techniques for transformation most effectively, one must first understand the nature of the mysterious "something" we call *consciousness,* that permeates all life. This section explains in clear, nontechnical language why the power of the mind is so effective in producing change in one's life. Rather than ask the reader to rely on faith alone in using these methods, data is presented from psychology, philosophy, and parapsychology to demonstrate how the mind functions, and how consciousness expresses itself in man as the life force behind all thought and action.

**PART II** is a practical handbook on how to apply the theory explained in **PART I**, and includes guided visualizations, self-healing techniques, affirmations to attract love and prosperity, and methods of inducing self-hypnosis.

If the reader is not interested in the philosophical discussion presented in **PART I** , he or she may skip this section and simply utilize the techniques given in **PART II**, either collectively, or singly, according to his or her preference.

# INTRODUCTION

*The greatest discovery of this
generation is that human beings
can alter their lives by altering
their attitude of mind.*
—*Albert Schweitzer*

As a psychotherapist in private practice, I see people daily who have created havoc in their lives through the misuse of their emotions. And I have seen the same people turn their lives around dramatically through contacting the tremendous power within them and using it constructively.

The greatest power in the world is inside your own head! It's called the subconscious mind. The ability to program correctly this incredible force within you can transform your personality and create miracles in your life. Knowledge of the dynamics of your subconscious mind can bring you perfect health, unlimited prosperity, self-confidence, peace of mind, loving relationships, and anything else you desire in your life. Used incorrectly or ignorantly, that same fantastic power can produce an existence of living hell. It all depends on your ability to program correctly this tremendously complex organ, the human brain, to bring you what you want in life, as well as your ability to deprogram it from the negative concepts that others have given you. In the realm of the subconscious, there is a *vital force* that can help and guide your life, if you will only listen to it, learn its laws, and program it correctly. Thus, *if you want to know what you've been asking for, just take a look at what you've got!*

We all determine the direction of our lives, but most of us do it unconsciously, and the consequence is often chaos. We create our own reality, and we are responsible for the things we attract into our lives through our own thinking processes. Through using your mind constructively, you can unlock dormant potentials within you, alter inappropriate behavior patterns, overcome the negative conditioning from your past and increase your creativity and self-confidence.

A biochemist whom I was counseling some years ago was a good example of how we can use the power of our subconscious mind to create a better life. Richard A. came to see me because of personal problems that were overwhelming him; he was particularly concerned because he had been searching for a job for over a month and had been unable to find one. This man was highly qualified, with a master's degree in chemistry, but his despondent attitude was preventing him from finding the position he so desperately wanted. I taught him how to make "money affirmations," a technique I learned from Leonard Orr, who teaches "Prosperity-consciousness" seminars in San Francisco. Since Richard was an intellectual and a scientist, he thought I was a little crazy to suggest that writing affirmations would get him the type of job he wanted, and at a high salary. Reluctantly, he carried out my suggestions. Within two weeks he found a job at a high-paying salary, with a large expense account and a company car.

Another client, Nancy K., a fifty-three year old divorced woman, had attempted for three years to find a man with whom she could spend her remaining years. After two disappointments in marriage, one lasting twenty-five years and the second, only a year and a half, she felt she was too old to attract the type of man she desired. Three years of making the rounds in the "singles scene" had left her already shaky self-esteem even more severely damaged, and she came to see me in a state of chronic depression.

After a few months of working on ways to increase her confidence and self-esteem, I taught Nancy how to use the power of her subconscious mind to attract into her life a suitable companion. She diligently applied these principles for several weeks, began to get telephone calls from men she had met in the past, and met new ones through friends who began inviting her to social affairs. Within a year she had met the right person and had remarried. Several months later I received a letter from her; she had moved to New York and was extremely happy, having at last found the fulfillment for which she had long been searching.

When I was twenty-one years of age, I enrolled in a course called Concept-Therapy. I was living in Toronto, Canada at the time, and was a shy, self-conscious, constantly-ill young woman with no belief in my own abilities. I managed to complete the course, but it took me three years to find the courage to enroll in the concomitant study group meetings. The first time I went to a meeting, there were only five other people present. Even so, when the textbook was passed so that each of us could read a paragraph from it aloud, I was too shy to do so and had to hand the book to the next person.

Learning more and more about the power of the mind, I decided to try imaging myself being more confident. I sat down every day, morning and evening, for about fifteen minutes, and concentrated all my energy on seeing myself standing before a group, perfectly poised and speaking clearly and confidently. The first step was to get the feeling over to my body that I really had the confidence I desired, which was very difficult because I had never experienced it. If I were a confident woman, I decided, I would probably hold my head up high, pull my shoulders back, and look other people directly in the eye. I walked around my apartment *acting as if* I had great self-confidence. A month after I began my imaging, the study group leader asked me to introduce the speaker at the next meeting, a meeting to be attended by some thirty people. And I did it! I was nervous, true, but I didn't fall to pieces; and I didn't lose my voice or faint, or suffer any of the other disasters I had previously anticipated. Delighted with my initial success, I continued visualizing myself as self-confident. By the time I moved from Canada to California, eight years later, I had conquered my inferiority complex to such an extent that I have now presented lectures to hundreds of people.

More and more people today are learning, as I so fortunately did early in my life, the methods for harnessing the tremendous power of the subconscious mind. The Astronaut, Captain Edgar Mitchell declared, "The simple secret of the universe is: you create your own reality! Deeply moved by his experience in outer space, he founded the Institute of Noetic Sciences in Palo Alto, California, and now devotes his life to research in parapsychology.

Your understanding of the profound significance of Captain Mitchell's few words can change your life dramatically. My objective in writing this book is to share with you a variety of techniques whereby you can utilize your potential to the fullest, and bcome as successful, happy, and prosperous as you want to be. Every one of us has mental powers and abilities that are lying dormant. We can awaken these by utilizing proven methods for getting in touch with the Great Power within us. These techniques are not new; they have been well-documented in the discipline of psychology, as well as in the lives of successful men and women who have learned the secret of tapping the inner power of the subconscious mind. Now you can join their ranks; all that is required is that you learn and apply the techniques for transformation set forth in this book.

Marta Hiatt,
San Jose,California,
August, 1988

3

**part one**

# THE
# EVOLUTION
# OF
# CONSCIOUSNESS

*Consciousness*
*must be a part of nature*
*or, more generally, of reality,*
*which means that,*
*quite apart from*
*the laws of physics and chemistry*
*as laid down in quantum theory,*
*we must also consider laws*
*of quite a different kind.*

*—Neils Bohr*
*Physics and Beyond*

# one

# ATTRIBUTES
# OF CONSCIOUSNESS

*Today there is a wide measure of agreement*
*which, on the physical side of science*
*approaches almost to unanimity,*
*that the stream of knowledge*
*is heading towards a non-mechanical reality;*
*the universe begins to look more like a great thought*
*than like a great machine.*

*—Werner Heisenburg*
*Physics and Beyond*

To use the techniques for transformation most effectively, we must first understand something of the nature of consciousness. To comprehend ourselves fully as beings in the world, we must necessarily attempt to understand this mysterious "something" we call consciousness, from its first manifestation in the world of matter, on up to the fully developed human being. Thus, we shall begin with a brief look at the atomic phase of creation because this is as far back as we can go to try to see what this Creative Power, manifesting in all of life, has been doing in its long evolutionary process on up to the creation of man. In order to understand our own nature, we have to go back to our ancient beginnings and examine the orderly process of creation. In so doing, we must necessarily consult the two authorities that have dealt extensively with this subject, science (which includes psychology), and theology, (which includes philosophy), since between them they embody all the knowledge we have about ourselves as beings in the universe.

## Consciousness in the Atomic Realm
Science states that, in the beginning, *if* there was a beginning, only atomic and subatomic particles existed. Science neither admits nor denies the existence of God, but merely states that, since God cannot be analyzed, tested or measured with physical instruments, the subject is not a fit study for scientific analysis. Thus, science ignores the question by giving us the theory of electronic particles as the starting point of all creation, and declares that it cannot go beyond that.

7

If we turn to theology with our inquiry about the beginning of creation, we are told that everything proceeded from the First Cause, God. Theology teaches that there was a definite, historical beginning to the universe, that God exists, and that this Being created the world. They claim that this theory requires no proof because the evidence resides simply in the fact that the universe is here and, since our minds cannot conceive of something being created out of nothing, it must therefore have been created by God. Certainly, all of our experience on earth indicates that every effect has its antecedent cause. Therefore, it seems logical that something must have set this cosmological process in motion, and something must be maintaining it. The question however, as to *what* that something is, is quite another matter!

In mentally constructing the beginning of the universe, we can conceive of a time when there was nothing but infinite space and, ultimately, this space became filled with countless electronic particles which eventually grouped together into atoms and molecules of matter. The question then is, "what Great Intelligence started this process eons ago eventually to form the universe, and what sustains it in its function?" At our present state of awareness and knowledge we can give only one answer: consciousness.

But, what is consciousness? No one really knows; but we do know some of the attributes of consciousness. Our definition is this: *Consciousness is the ability to receive and respond to impressions from outside stimuli.* Consciousness, therefore, is a state of *awareness*, no matter how minimal. And this ability exists even within the electron; thus, we can conclude that there is consciousness within all forms of matter, from submicroscopic particles of energy to man.

Within the atom, consciousness manifests itself in the form of attraction and repulsion. When two electrons (negative particles) are brought into proximity, they try to avoid each other; there appears to be a factor of recognition, a kind of "conscious knowledge" on an elemental level. Yet there is neither brain nor nervous system to register these impressions; it happens without any mental mechanism whatsoever. This suggests that electrons possess an attribute of consciousness, a type of *receptivity* in a very fundamental form. Like particles repel each other, and a field is set up whereby they try to move out of the way of each other. But how do they recognize another particle as being either positive or negative, without sensory equipment to record these impressions? The only answer is that the electrons have consciousness on an elemental level.

According to an article in SCIENTIFIC AMERICAN 251:50-58, 1985, the existence of "memory" at the atomic level has now been demonstrated. According to physicists Richard Brewer and Erwin Hahn, "atomic memory" is evident when atomic systems that have moved from order into chaos are induced to recover their initial order. The two scientists showed how a system of particles decayed from a highly ordered state can be returned to that state simply by reversing the motion of its particles.

If consciousness is in every atom and atoms are present in every cell, it follows, therefore, that consciousness is present throughout our cellular human bodies. This is what we mean by saying we are alive; it is this consciousness that is flowing through us and sustaining us. *Consciousness is the one and only reality in the universe*, and it manifests Itself through different forms.

We postulate that the universe began with these subatomic particles floating around in outer space and then, gradually, over eons of time, they began to group together and, as a result, the physical universe came into being. It is only logical to assume that this did not happen as the result of a giant cosmological accident, as some scientists think, but that this Creative Force within the electronic particles must have had some plan of operation in the construction of the universe, as we see an incredible order and harmony manifest throughout it. We hypothesize from this that the material universe is the result of an *image* projected by this Creative Power, whatever It may be. The image, therefore, is one manifestation of consciousness and, Chapter 6 demonstrates how to use this attribute to effect changes in your life through mental visualization, a technique for transformation.

Our hypothesis, then, is that there is an extant Creative Force, which we call *consciousness,* which evolved the natural universe out of Itself and which is the vital energy maintaining and sustaining everything in existence. Given this premise, let us briefly examine the nature of this Force as it manifests Itself in the universe so that we can discover some of Its other attributes. To do this we will progressively examine the evolution of consciousness as depicted in the following chart.

**Consciousness in the Mineral Realm**

Thomas Payne stated, "The only evidence you will ever get of the Creative Power is from studying nature", so that is where we will begin our quest for an understanding of life. If we start by examining the mineral phase of creation, which is on the lower end of the

9

# THE EVOLUTION OF CONSCIOUSNESS

| THE ALL | ATOMIC | MINERAL | PLANT | ANIMAL | HUMAN | COSMIC | THE ALL |
|---------|--------|---------|-------|--------|-------|--------|---------|
| **X** | | (DIATOM) | (EUGLENA) | (APE) | (CHRIST) (BUDDHA) (SOCRATES) | | **?** |
| | INORGANIC LIFE | ELEMENTS | CELLULAR LIFE | | | IMMORTALITY | |
| IMAGE | | | | | | | |
| | ATTRACTION / REPULSION | ORGANIZATION | ADAPTATION | LOCOMOTION INSTINCT | SELF-AWARENESS, REFLECTIVE THOUGHT, REASON | INTUITIVE AWARENESS | ONENESS |

CONSCIOUSNESS — SPIRIT

evolutionary continuum, we discover another attribute of consciousness: each mineral is crystalized according to a definite design or image. There are many different kinds of crystals, but the pattern for the particular shape that each one will take is embedded within its atomic structure. The pattern of a quartz crystal, for instance, is a basic idea, an image in nature which can be repeated again and again. Just as the pattern, or image, of the oak tree is within the tiny acorn, so too is the image of the human being contained within the microscopic DNA strands of the fertilized egg in the mother's womb. When you were so tiny that it would have required an electronic microscope to find you, the blueprint, or image, for the color of your eyes, the thickness of your hair, the structure of your bones, and all of your other physical characteristics, was already established. And, as we will try to show, the divine plan of our lives is also incorporated into that blueprint, for us to discover through introspection and meditation.

The question naturally arises: where did the basic pattern for a quartz crystal, or an oak tree, or a human being originate? To any thinking person it is clear that some kind of intelligent force, which we call consciousness, must have projected an image which ultimately manifested itself as a particular created form.

The first principle of all creation is that everything begins with a plan, or image. If you were to build a house, you would naturally begin with a plan, a blueprint. It is the same with building a life, but very few people are aware of the necessity of having a definite plan for their lives. Consequently, they are floundering about and don't know where they are going, or why. It makes no difference what you want to accomplish; you must start with a clear image of your objective and, the more perfect your idea, the more perfect will be your creation. Conversely, the sloppier your idea, the sloppier the result!

**Consciousness in the Plant Realm**

Advancing along the evolutionary continuum to the next stage of creation, vegetation, we discover the presence of consciousness in the phenomenon of photosynthesis. This process of plants manufacturing their own food by utilizing sunlight indicates that there is a vital intelligence within the organism. In the plant phase of creation, we are now dealing for the first time with *cellular life*, a vastly significant advance in consciousness.

One of the chief characteristics that plants exhibit, which is not found in inorganic material, is the ability to adapt. A tiny fern, for example, will grow up through concrete or tar if it must. A potato in a dark cellar somehow discerns the direction of light and turns it sprouts that way. A cutting from certain plants, such as a geranium, if planted, will adapt to its new situation and develop specialized root cells where there were none before. This is a high degree of adaptation, and this principle applies to the human realm as well as the plant.

*The greater the ability to adapt, the higher the consciousness within a form.* The organism that survives is always the one that has the ability to adapt itself to its environment. Saplings bend in the wind; otherwise they will snap in two. Unfortunately, however, many human beings have not developed the attribute of adaptability; they resist their circumstances and become unyielding towards life. Neurotic people, for example, characteristically develop a rigid way of reacting to every situation. They cannot deviate from their inflexible behavior pattern no matter what the circumstances, so they are defeated by their inability to adapt and devise more effective ways of responding to life.

The attribute of *adaptability* is characteristic of the mature, psychologically healthy person. In fact, we could say that rigidity equals pathology, and fluidity equals health, in both the physical and mental realms. In this tense, stress-filled world, those who survive without breaking down are people who are capable of making the necessary adjustments to the changes wrought by ever more sophisticated technology. If a person rigidly and continually resists change, he or she will be broken by life, just as a resisting tree can be broken by a powerful wind.

Though consciousness expresses itself in various forms there is really no fixed dividing line between the different phases of creation, just a gradual blending as consciousness begins expressing itself through higher and more complex models. An example of this gradual transition is the euglena, a green aquatic plant that manufactures its own food through photosynthesis, as plants normally do. When the euglena is in darkness, however, the green coloration temporarily disappears; and it propels itself by its flagellum through the water, feeding on bacteria. Locomotion and digestion of animal matter are characteristics of the next highest phase of creation, the animal realm, so we might say that the euglena is a "missing link" between the plant and animal kingdoms.

**Consciousness in the Animal Realm**

As every animal lover knows, animals can perform some truly remarkable feats even though they lack the fully developed reason of the human being. Consciousness expresses itself in this phase of the evolutionary continuum through *instinct,* and instinct in the animal realm is a perfect guide. It is instinct which leads the wild duck to sense the coming of winter and to fly thousands of miles from its home in the north to a little pond in a warmer climate—the exact same pond that its ancestors landed on the year before, and the year before that, ad infinitum.

A bee cannot fly, according to the science of aerodynamics, for its body is too bulky for its delicate wings. Fortunately, the bee does not know this; so it buzzes from flower to flower, guided entirely by instinct. And certain crustaceans and echinoderms, such as the lobster and starfish, are guided by instinct to grow a new limb if one is lost.

While instinct is a perfect guide for an animal, it cannot be improved upon, so an animal is locked into what it already knows; it must keep performing the same actions in the same ways, just as all of its forebears have done for centuries. But mankind is not doomed to such repetitious behavior for, in addition to instinct, we possess the highest quality that consciousness manifests, *self-awareness.*

## Consciousness in the Human Realm

Self-awareness, or reflective thought, is the main attribute that distinguishes man from the animal. This is the consciousness that enables us to think inwardly, to contemplate ourselves; for reflection is the power to turn one's consciousness upon oneself, to know oneself and, especially, *to know that one knows.* A human is the only creation in the universe who is the object of his own reflection and, because of that, another world is born: an inner world, which is a reality in which no lower animal can ever participate. Incapable of contemplating itself, or of being aware of itself as the conscious subject, not even a higher type of animal, such as a dog or cat, that knows where its master is and where its food is, can know that it knows. In consequence, it is denied access to a whole domain of reality in which man can move freely. Systems of physics, philosophy, mathematics, and astronomy, for example, have all been constructed because of man's unique ability to reflect inwardly. Because of this new attribute, *self-awareness,* we have a host of expanded abilities: abstract reasoning, free will, creative ability, foresight in order to plan ahead, and many others.

It is indeed a great treasure to be aware of oneself. And, since this is the characteristically human quality, the more aware one is, the more fully developed a human being is.

In this vast evolutionary process we see consciousness expanding itself through the perfecting of exquisitely complex and efficient nervous systems and, especially, in the formation and development of the human brain. Man's highly perfected brain is the center of consciousness, and consciousness is the heart of evolution; it is the Creative Force Itself, for we are each "consciousness in expression."

Our criterion or measurement of advanced self-consciousness therefore, is self-awareness, the ability to think inwardly, to reflect upon oneself, to contemplate one's inner nature. Thus, if this is the indication of a higher type of consciousness, it follows that *the greater the ability for self-reflection and self-awareness, the more advanced the consciousness,* or the more evolved the soul. A highly developed person, such as Socrates, for example, would spend a great deal of time contemplating inwardly to get in touch with his or her inner self. If we examine the lives of all great thinkers, we will discover that they set aside some time each day for inner reflection, which is the most direct path to higher consciousness. If you wish to know who you really are, you must stop long enough to reflect upon yourself. The importance of meditation will be discussed in Chapter 5.

Since the animal has only *simple* consciousness and does not have *self*-awareness or *self*-consciousness, its consciousness is always directed outwardly toward finding food, mating, avoiding enemies, etc. However, even in the least evolved human being; for example, the primitive bushman, there is at least a faint degree of the inward direction of consciousness, or reflective thought. Man can intellectualize; he can conceptualize; he can analyze experiences and compare them with previous ones. Mankind, the most marvelous life form in the universe and the apex of creation, has risen from the animal plane of simple consciousness to self-consciousness!.

There are three levels or types of consciousness, as represented by the following diagram. A newborn human baby begins life on the border between animal and human consciousness. It has the potential for self-consciousness and reflective thought, but these qualities are not yet developed. At a certain stage in the child's maturation—approximately two or three years old—it begins to become aware of itself as a separate entity, and the sense of separateness is born. The child is becoming humanized.

But there is a price to pay for this increased consciousness, because human anxiety is directly connected to the advent of self-reflection. And the price is this: *the more we know, the more we desire; and the more we desire, the more we suffer from the pain of wanting and not having.*. Buddha stated that all suffering was caused by desire, thus, the more one can eliminate desire, the closer one will come to the state of bliss, or perfect happiness.

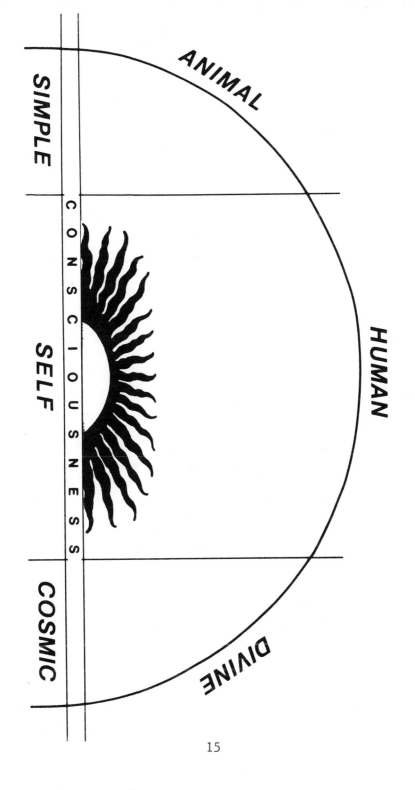

The problem with man's evolution is that we have not yet learned how to use our newly developed gift, rational thought, wisely. We have not been taught properly how to reason, and how to handle our emotions constructively. In psychology, philosophy, and theology, the three systems which should be able to teach us how to live, there is enormous confusion, contradiction, and contention.

Because we have the power of choice, the human consciousness is the only form that can work against the inherent plan within it. The power of choice implies a tremendous responsibility, and some of us obviously have been choosing irresponsibly, judging by the state of the world. If a person makes choices which interfere with or go contrary to the consciousness within, that interference will always manifest itself externally in one's life. It was only when self-consciousness began to develop, with its singular power of originating ideas, that many of the various forms of disease appeared.

The animal realm is guided solely by instinct, and therefore it cannot interfere with the perfect operation of the Power Within. Because of this, the animal kingdom is free from all of the various diseases that plague mankind. In the animal realm there are only some dozen or so diseases to which animals left to themselves out in nature are subject. In the human realm there are over three thousand different disease categories. And what is the major difference between the human and animal worlds? The ability to reason abstractly. Obviously, something has been wrong with the way we have used our reasoning ability because man's world is filled with strife, violence, and mental and physical illnesses.

Human beings are suspended between the animal and divine phases of evolution, but we have the capacity to attain to even greater heights of consciousness. Some people are developing towards their highest expression but, unfortunately, many others are actually retrogressing and becoming more animalistic than any beast.

In developing self-consciousness, man has not achieved the ultimate goal, for our destiny as human beings is to continue to evolve toward *cosmic consciousness*. Remember that a division between one phase of evolution and another is not rigidly defined; the chart is a heuristic model to demonstrate that there is a continuum of consciousness and that this whole complement is latent within each of us, waiting for us to discover it. Now that we are in the universe, a part of us is here forever, because the Law of Conservation of Energy states that energy can neither be created nor destroyed. When we die, the atoms of our physical bodies merely change form, returning to the earth, but our consciousness, the Spirit within us which is a part of the All, continues its manifest destiny of evolution.

16

Each one of us is a part of the all-pervasive consciousness of the universe, and our ultimate evolution is beyond the powers of the imagination! That self-same consciousness is also the power that is sustaining you, and it can be contacted and directed when you understand Its laws. This, then, is our great task in life, and that is what life is all about: the attainment of unity with the All. In order to achieve this it is necessary to learn how to think properly and how to channel our emotions into constructive ends. We have the freedom to go against our own purpose for being, our own innate plan, our inner image. We can interfere with it and cause chaos, and that inner disharmony is always manifested, either in the body through physical illness, in the mind through neurotic or psychotic symptoms, or externally in confusion and unhappiness in our lives. What we must learn is how to make the right choices for our lives that are in harmony with the great cosmological plan. In order to do that we need to understand how Consciousness, the great Creative Power of the Universe, operates within human personality; how our minds become programmed to ideas, and how to change these ideas if they are destructive. We will explore these areas in the chapters to follow.

*I want to demonstrate that*
*spiritual values have naturalistic meaning*
*that they are not the exclusive possession*
*of organized churches*
*that they do not need supernatural concepts*
*to validate them,*
*that they are well within the jurisdiction*
*of a suitably enlarged science,*
*and that, therefore, they are the general*
*responsibility of ALL mankind.*
*—Abraham H. Maslow*

# two

# THE GREAT POWER WITHIN YOU

*Everyone who is seriously involved*
*in the pursuit of science*
*becomes convinced that a Spirit*
*is manifest in the Laws of the Universe—*
*A Spirit vastly superior to that of man,*
*and one in the face of which we,*
*with our modest powers,*
*must feel humble.*
*—Albert Einstein*

### Spirit Within: The Creative Power of the Universe

Having explored the attributes of consciousness in the previous chapters, we will now examine how consciousness expresses itself in human personality. Consciousness, or the highest part of man, has been called by many names. The New Testament gospels speak of it as "the Kingdom of Heaven within a man," 'the mustard seed," "the pearl of great price." The Muslims call it "the secret," and say it is closer to man than breathing. In chinese wisdom it is "the Jewel," "the Diamond Center," "the Pearl that the dragons guard." The Roman emperor, Marcus Aurelius, wrote that it is "a source of strength which will always spring up if thou wilt look within." Plotinus called it "the Soul-Center;" others have called it "the Oversoul." The chiropractor names it "the Innate Mind," the psychologist, "the Unconscious." But, say the Taoists, "the name that can be named is not the eternal name." Anything, then, that we can say about this Power must necessarily be symbolic; even those who have had a transcendent, mystical experience have not the words to describe it.

18

We now want to show how Spirit expresses Itself in human personality. In our understanding of life, we usually put science in one corner and theology in another, but their differences are not as extreme as we have assumed; there is an integration between some of the tenets of both approaches to this mystery of life. To demonstrate this theoretical integration, we will use both the theological and psychological terms for understanding human personality. Psychology has divided the mind theoretically into two parts, the conscious and subconscious (or unconscious). To show the correlation between the psychological and theological teachings, we will use these terms, but we will also use the religious term, soul, for the conscious part of the mind, and Spirit for the subconscious. We use the term Spirit to represent that Unknowable Power that first manifested Itself in electronic particles, and is now manifesting in us, and this name is synonymous with consciousness. Although Spirit is all-pervasive in the universe, in human personality It seems to have Its central locus within the subconscious realm. It operates on the unconscious level and takes care of all our bodily functions, such as beating our heart, and circulating our blood.

Spirit has been with us since the moment of conception when a single cell of life was created and we were just a tiny speck of matter smaller than the head of a pin. The question therefore is: when those two cells united to form a microscopic cell, was that *you*? Were you there? If a human being consists of body, mind and soul, as most of have been taught through traditional religion, none of these could have been present at your conception. There was certainly no body developed, and there could be no mind because the mind is dependent upon the brain, and the brain was not yet formed. As to the existence of the soul at conception, we must turn to the scriptural definition which states: "God breathed into man's nostrils the breath of life; and man became a living soul." (Genesis 2:7) Since there were no nostrils at conception, and no "breathing," if we accept this statement literally, the soul had not yet developed.

If *you* were not there, then what was there? Logical reasoning offers only one answer: The Great Unknowable Power, Spirit, must have been there. *Some* type of consciousness had to be present in that single microscopic cell to develop you into an embryo, create all the organs, the tremendously intricate brain and spinal cord, and all the other incredible complexities of your fully-formed body. Spirit was within you at the moment of conception, and then It divided each cell again and again until, in the short space of approximately 280 days, you emerged comprised of some 63 trillion cells. And every one of those cells, from first to last, contains Spirit, just as every cell of your adult body still contains the Creative Power of the universe. Consider for a moment, the great wonder of this!

And here is another unfathomable mystery: the DNA strands, which contain the blueprint of the baby-to-be, are within the nucleus of each cell, and they replicate themselves when a cell divides. Even though each cell duplicates itself exactly, soon certain cells begin to specialize, becoming heart cells or hair cells or skin cells. How do they do this? How do they know what they are supposed to become since they are all alike? No one knows, but it is obvious they must be directed by an *intelligent consciousness*, which we call Spirit.

Because Spirit is in all of our cells, It is responsible for keeping our bodies functioning normally. The conscious mind cannot perform physiological tasks because it does not know how. If your conscious mind had to beat your heart for the next three minutes, for example, you would die because you would not know how to get blood up to your brain. Consider, for example, that you could not walk if you had to do it with your conscious, reasoning mind; for you do not know what muscles to use, and in what sequence and with what exertion, in order to keep from falling on your face!

Or, consider a mother who gives her milk to her baby. What happens next? The mother doesn't know how to turn milk into blood and bones and lymph and everything else her baby needs in order to grow; and neither does the baby. We can recognize from this that we are dealing with a Conscious Entity within us; there is consciousness experiencing all of life, and it is experiencing a little part of it through that baby, and through you. Think of it—the Creative Power of the universe resides within your own being!

Spirit will take care of our bodies perfectly as long as we don't interfere with It. If our heart or liver or digestive system is not functioning properly (unless there is a genetic disorder), somehow we have interrupted the orderly direction of the Power within through incorrect thinking, improper care of the body, or misuse of our emotions. If you have inadvertently created some dis-ease within your body, you can correct it, for the *power that made your body can heal your body.* You will learn how to do this in Chapter Ten on Self-healing, because this Power within can be contacted and directed if we understand Its laws.

Spirit is all-pervasive in the universe; there is something beyond the little ego-self, and the effect of discovering It will transform and elevate and re-create the life of the one who knows it. Utilizing this knowledge is the means by which a person becomes their true self.

20

And when someone understands that, they usually begin to serve as an instrument for this Creative Power to help uplift the consciousness of the world. When the realization fully dawns upon a person that Spirit, the Creative Power of the Universe, resides within their own being, they become sublimely able to handle any problems and to transform their life and relationships, because this Power is an active, dynamic Force that can be consciously directed, and It will do whatever we ask of It.

The great psychologist Carl Jung wrote that "The decisive question for man is: Is he related to something infinite or not? That is the telling question of his life. Only if we know that the thing which truly matters is the Infinite can we avoid fixing our interest upon futilities, and upon all kinds of goals which are not of real importance. If we understand and feel that right here in this life we already have a link with the Infinite, then our desires and attitudes change." Jung was a discerning man who recognized that human anxiety is directly traceable to a longing to be reunited with the Divine Source of one's being. And that is what everyone is looking for through various means, although It may be called by different names.

Occasionally, someone knocks at my door to ask, "Do you believe in God?" What that person is really asking is, "Do you believe in *my concept* of God?" No one can believe in anyone else's God; the only God you will ever know is the one you come to identify personally with; the one that you discover through an individual, inner experience within the silence of your own heart. That is the only God that can ever exist for you, and It can never be discovered by the intellect alone. We can call this Power God, or Jehovah, Allah, Nature, Infinite Mind, Almighty Being, the All, or a host of other appellations; but what is important to realize is that Spirit is *within*. And, that it is not a domineering, authoritarian, capricious, wrathful entity, as God is so often depicted by unenlightened clerics, but rather It is an active, beneficent, and creative Power.

We therefore posit that there are four aspects to human personality: body, mind, soul, and Spirit. This theory departs from traditional religion which teaches there are only three aspects—body, mind, and soul—and places Spirit (or God) outside human personality, residing somewhere in the heavens. This is the great error in those teachings, for the Creative Intelligence is *within us,* just as It is within everything else in the universe.

God is not locked up in some church building, and one does not have to be in a specific place to revere Life. God is not formal; you don't have to wear a jacket and a hat in order to commune with the

Divine Presence, which is ever-present. God is not solemn and does not have to be approached with a long face and a bowed head. And God is not invisible. If we merely open our minds and eyes, we will see that all of life is but a manifestation of this *One Consciousness,* through different forms. As Walt Whitman put it: *Every moment of the light and dark is a miracle, every cubic inch of space is a miracle.*

Whenever we are moved by the higher aspect of our being, such as when we are listening to a beautiful piece of music, feeling love towards someone, or watching a lovely sunset, we are in contact with our higher self. And this is what all our yearnings really are, the longing to reunite with Spirit. "Our hearts are restless," said St. Augustine, "till they rest in Thee."

**The Ego and Self-Identity: What is the Soul?**

As noted before, psychology has theoretically divided the mind into two aspects, and what we call Spirit is what the psychologist calls the unconscious, or subconscious mind. For the conscious aspect of the mind, we will also use another term from theology, soul.

For centuries much controversy has raged about the meaning of the term soul, primarily around the question: "Do I have a soul, or am I a soul?" In Genesis 2:7 it is written that "the Lord God breathed into man's nostrils the breath of life, and man *became* a living soul." According to that passage, the soul must be something that one *is*, not something that one possesses. Yet many followers of traditional religion think of the soul as a possession that they are in danger of losing; a nebulous, ghost-like entity that will float up to heaven (or down to hell) at death. This is a very childish notion and one that has been abandoned by more advanced thinkers.

The soul is not a thing that you can own, but an expression of your personality, or a form of consciousness. But, when does one become a soul? When does God "breathe the breath of life" into a person? When does this universal consciousness arrive at a point where we call it a soul? People have tried to answer this question in a number of ways, and it has even been fought on the floor of the United States Congress. Some say it is about five months after conception when the fetus takes its first breath in the mother's womb; it moves and its heart beats. And some say it occurs after about three months when the embryo is fully formed. Others insist that the soul appears at the very moment of conception, and there are those who say the soul appears when the baby is born and it takes its first breath of fresh air.

So what is the answer to this dilemma? The problem is that the question is phrased incorrectly. The soul is not "born" at some

22

particular moment in time because it is not a fixed state of being but a state of *becoming*. Soul is synonymous with personality, representing the conscious part of it. Therefore, it is not something that leaps into the baby's body at some historical point, but something which gradually emerges as the baby matures. If we want to use the word *born,* we would say that the soul is born when *self*-consciousness appears, for this is the main attribute of the soul. Until this occurs, the soul exists only in potential.

When a human baby is born, it is on much the same plane as the animal, for it is not a fully developed, distinct personality until it has awareness of itself as an individual; that is, when self-consciousness has developed. Up to that point we might say that a newborn baby is a latent soul, or an expression of pure Spirit.

The soul, or personality, develops as a result of the interaction of its inherited characteristics and environment, which produces behavior, and it is this behavior, which includes cognitive processes, that we call personality. Before this interaction begins, usually between the ages of three and seven, the child has only the potential for self-consciousness. Maturation over a period of time is required for the emergence of a structured personality, and the full development of the soul. Most people realize their full potentiality only upon reaching early adulthood, for the development of the soul necessarily depends upon the acquisition of two important human attributes, rational thought, and symbolic verbal skills. If these two abilities do not develop properly, the person will have a very restrained, limited, and restricted personality, or expression of soul. As Barbara Branden stated in her lecture on Efficient Thinking: "Language is the only form in which it is possible to reason explicitly, and to subject one's conclusions to the judgement of reason and reality. In order to think man has to draw abstractions, to form concepts, and to give these concepts identity by means of specific words."

For our purposes then, the definition of the soul is this: *it is the individual's unique organization of inherited characteristics and environmental influences, which result in consistent behavior patterns.* The soul is the organizing function within the individual and the means by which one human being can relate to another. So the soul is not a possession and not a thing; it is not a constant, or fixed entity, because it is always growing, changing, and evolving.

The soul is that aspect of your consciousness that can originate ideas, think, intellectualize, and reason. It is the *individualized* aspect of Spirit and is therefore different in everyone. Spirit is the *universal* aspect of the personality and is the same in everyone. Soul represents our sense of personal self-identity as it expresses itself uniquely through each person. Each soul is different, of course, because every person has a different genetic and environmental history.

In the development of the human brain we now have for the first time in evolutionary history the division of consciousness into two parts. (Represented by a division of the line of Consciousness on the evolutionary chart). Consciousness then, is no longer singular as it is in the lower phases of the evolutionary continuum; man has a dual nature, and consciousness manifests in us as soul and Spirit, or the conscious and subconscious minds. Reflective thought requires that division of consciousness, for one aspect must be able to reflect upon the other. Logic and reason are the predominant characteristics of the conscious mind, and emotion and intuition are those of the subconscious. These different aspects have their separate physiological correlates in the right and left hemispheres of the brain, and function oppositionally.

Another point we should be aware of is that the soul must always have some form through which to express itself, and that form on this plane of existence is the physical body. We can only recognize other people because they are expressing themselves through a physical medium; otherwise, they would have no personality or existence. Form is an attribute of consciousness; and all manifestations of consciousness have form. Does this mean then, that the soul is gone once the physical body is gone? No, but it does mean that the soul must express itself through some other form; otherwise it would have no continuing existence. In metaphysics this other form is called the astral or etheric body, which man is said to possess along with the physical body.

We must realize that the soul and body do not act as separate entities; the organism functions as a single unity, and what happens to a part always affects the whole. Every thought we think produces an immediate physiological response, for the relationship between soul and body is intimate in the extreme. The body is certainly a part of our personality, the most evident part; and we would have no self-identity without our physical identity. Certainly, our self-image is greatly influenced by the condition of our physical state.

Souls, or personalities, are at different stages of development; some are very advanced; others, very deficient and functioning at a minimal level. Not all adults achieve full maturity; some remain almost infantile in their expression, and we could say that they have a restricted personality, or a limited soul development. Many people are not even remotely aware of their higher nature and they rush through life operating by conditioned reflex, just like an animal. Such people never raise their consciousness much above that of the beast, and the spark of divinity within them remains dormant for the whole of their lives.

It is the task of each of us to awaken the divine spark within, thereby first attaining to individual consciousness, and then to unity with Spirit. That is what being a soul really means. It may seem incredible that some people have not yet even reached individual consciousness, but this is actually their level of development. They are entirely reactive beings; they have very little free will because they just give programmed responses to environmental stimuli, without thinking or reasoning about their reactions. They are little more than talking animals, and they live out their lives largely unconsciously. Sometimes their subconscious mind, which is always striving towards growth, has to totally disrupt the lives of these limited people in order to open them up to their potentialities.

The great task of our lives, and the duty of every man and woman, is to work at increasing our self-awareness and freeing ourselves from the enslavement of past conditioning. Our task is to become cognizant of the fact that we are a part of the Infinite, and to begin expressing this higher consciousness through our personalities. It is only when there is some measure of synthesis established between the conscious and subconscious aspects of an individual's being that he or she begins to establish a true identity as a person and becomes a soul. Only then is a person fully awakened.

## three

# REPROGRAMMING THE MIND

*In our unconscious mind we cannot
distinguish between a wish and a deed.*
—Freud

Soul and Spirit, conscious and subconscious mind: how do these two aspects of man's dual nature work together? How do we get programmed to the various concepts which govern us, and how can we reprogram our minds to eliminate negative ideas so that we may live happily and productively?

The diagram on the next page illustrates the division of the mind. Of course Spirit flows through both aspects of the mind, but It is partially shut off from our conscious awareness by a *psychic barrier*, or psychic censor, which prevents us from having complete contact with the subconscious mind. This barrier is semi-permeable because the soul can never operate entirely independently of Spirit, and its manifestation is always an interactionary process. Because this barrier is partly open, and not solid, we often get messages from our inner self, in the form of intuitive insights, dreams, or precognition of events. It is because of this psychic barrier that individuality is possible. If this division of consciousness did not exist, we would all be the same and have no distinct personality, nor self-awareness. Certain differences in temperament might exist, as they do in the animal world, due to genetic predispositions, but there would not be a sense of identity, a self-image, or rational thinking, all of which are aspects of our personality.

As stated earlier, soul is the conscious part of our personality, the part that originates the ideas which will manifest in our life, or accepts ideas from others. These concepts then lodge in our subconscious mind, and it is the subconscious which carries them out. Soul, therefore, is the *thinker*. It can also be considered the originative, "masculine" aspect of the self, as it implants ideas in the subconscious mind.

Spirit, the subconscious, is the *doer,* the receptive, "feminine" aspect, since It receives the ideas and carries them out. This is the same creative principle at work in the realm of the mind as it is in the biological world: the masculine, originative soul impregnates the

26

feminine, receptive Spirit with an idea; and the creation that results from this interaction is the physical expression, or behavior.

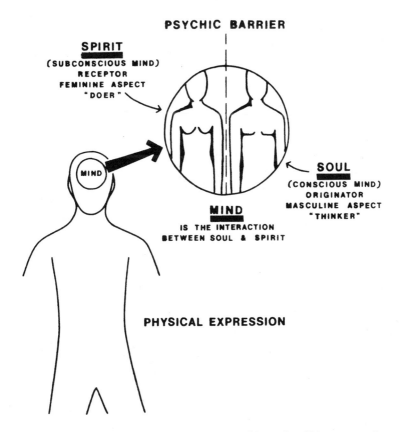

Let us say that the soul originates the idea of walking somewhere. It can consciously think up this idea, but it actually has no power to carry it out since it does not know which muscles are involved in the simple act of taking a step. So it must turn its idea over to Spirit, the formative aspect, which then activates the many muscles involved. Walking is the behavior which results from this interchange.

We speak colloquially of the subconscious and the conscious mind, but what is mind? The mind is not a thing; it is a function, a process; and it has no existence in and of itself. Mind is a term used to describe the action of the cells, neurons, and chemical processes of the brain. It is simply the name given to the interaction between soul and Spirit: the process of thinking. Unlike the soul, which is the organizing factor within the personality, and thus an entity in itself, the mind is a temporary, fleeting phenomenon which is dependent entirely upon stimuli from the internal and external environment.

In order for the process of thinking to occur, the five senses must transmit some sort of impression to the soul, which takes that information and passes it on to Spirit Within. Spirit then matches the impression with one of the patterns in Its vast data bank and flashes that back to the soul, which is then able to interpret the particular vibration (or wave length) that it has picked up from its perceptual senses. This interaction between conscious and subconscious is instantaneous, of course, and it is the process we call thinking.

Scientifically, what occurs is that the firing of certain neurons in the brain reaches a "critical level of awareness," which causes a person to become conscious of a particular vibration. Each part of the brain is always at a certain level of alertness; there are always some neurons firing somewhere in the brain, so the cells are in a constant state of vibration. When certain neurons fire above this critical level, the neural processes are consciously experienced, and we have a thought about something. Mind is the name given to this activity of the brain cells; therefore it is that portion of your consciousness which is above a critical level of alertness or vibration at a given time. Or, we could say that the amplitude, or strength, of the vibration of particular cells and neurons increases when coming in contact with stimuli resonating to their vibration.

For example, let us say you are strolling along the street and pass a bakery. Stimuli will be received through your olfactory sense, or sense of smell. At that moment a vibration will be picked up which will be in resonance with certain cells of your brain which are related to that stimuli, and neurons will begin firing. When their amplitude becomes heightened above a critical level, you will have a thought that there is fresh bread baking in that store; and then you will have to decide whether to buy some bread or not.

Every experience we have ever had is impressed somewhere on electrochemical cells in our brain. This is our storehouse of memory; akin to an enormous data bank. Every time the soul receives a stimulus and requests information about it from Spirit, Spirit instantly activates this computer bank, and fires the associated brain neurons to identify the experience so that you can interpret it for what it is. Dr. William Penfield's experiments at McGill University, probing the brain with electrodes, proved that everything we have ever seen, heard, smelled, touched, or tasted is imprinted on our brain cells forever. Whenever something reactivates those cells, we get a mental and emotional picture duplicating the original experience, although the emotional intensity decreases with the passage of time.

But, what happens if you hear about, or see, something of which you have no knowledge? Since lm impression has been been registered on the cells of your brain, Spirit will simply provide you with a related, or associated, picture.

## How Our Minds Become Programmed

The conscious part of our mind has two types of processes available to it, induction and deduction. The subconscious, on the other hand, can only function deductively. This fact is of enormous importance in understanding how the mind works, as these processes operate quite differently,

Only the conscious mind has the ability to distinguish between constructive and destructive concepts; an ability not always used with great perspicacity; for too often the soul unwittingly originates or accepts negative concepts which eventually will impact or control her life. So we will begin the process of reprogramming our mind to constructive thoughts by examining the way negative concepts lodge in our subconscious. An understanding of this will enable you to reprogram Spirit with the concepts you want in your life and to eliminate negative ones you may have already acquired.

Inductive reasoning, which is *solely* a function of the conscious mind, involves analyzing, judging, and selecting when you assemble a number of disparate ideas to compare. This involves *thinking,* a function *only* of the conscious mind. For example, when you enter a meeting room, you choose a place to sit by using inductive reasoning. You may want to sit by a window, or near a friend, or in a comfortable chair, or close to the chalkboard. You examine the possibilities, analyze them, and select the one which best suits your criteria. Induction starts with isolated ideas and determines the common relationship of them all; it moves from specifics to the general. It is not necessarily concerned with reaching a conclusion, only with the acceptability of each separate idea.

Deductive functioning, which does not involve reasoning, can also be used by the conscious mind, but it is the *only* method available to the subconscious. The evidence that the subconscious mind functions deductively is provided by hypnosis. In this altered state of consciousness, a hypnotist talks directly to the subconscious mind of a subject without interference from the rational, conscious portion of the subject's mind. As has been well-documented, in the hypnotic state subjects can produce phenomena which would be difficult, if not

29

impossible, during the normal, fully-conscious state. Subjects, for example, have been observed to maintain cataleptic postures for hours without discomfort, to enjoy a glass of vinegar thinking it is tea, and to have needles stuck in their flesh without feeling pain, among other affects. These abnormal phenomena are produced because, in hypnosis, the subconscious of the subject accepts the suggestions of the hypnotist without reasoning or questioning them, which indicates the receptive, passive unquestioning, non-analytical nature of the subconscious mind.

An understanding of how Spirit, or the subconscious, operates, is necessary in order to reprogram your mind to positive concepts. Generally speaking, deduction starts with given premises and leads to a conclusion. A premise is simply a statement; it can be true or false. Two premises, a major and a minor premise, plus a conclusion deduced from them, construct what is known in logic and metaphysics as a syllogism. The conclusion is colored, of course, by whether the premises are true or not; but the important point is: the subconscious cannot judge the veracity of the premises; it can only draw a conclusion from the given data. Here is a classic example of a syllogism:

| | |
|---|---|
| Major premise: | All trees have roots. |
| Minor premise: | An oak is a tree. |
| Therefore: | An oak has roots. |

When the soul (or someone else, such as a parent) originates the premises through a suggestion, it turns them over to Spirit, which draws a conclusion and operates on the basis of that conclusion, true or false. Since Spirit cannot judge the accuracy of the premises or reject them if they are false, It has no choice but to accept and execute them. Obviously, if you give Spirit false premises, you will get an erroneous conclusion. If you give Spirit premises which are harmful or destructive to you, you will be harmed or even destroyed by the conclusion you force Spirit to act out. Remember, *Spirit cannot reason;* that is solely an ability of the conscious mind.

Let's look at a few samples of these injurious syllogisms which are so commonplace that we often let Spirit incorporate them without thinking about the consequences.

1. Major premise: If you get your feet wet you'll catch a cold.
   Minor premise: My feet are wet.
   Therefore: I will catch a cold.


2. Major premise: Women can't earn a lot of money.
   Minor premise: I am a woman.
   Therefore: I can't earn a lot of money.


3. Major premise: My father had a heart attack.
   Minor premise: I am just like my father.
   Therefore: I will have a heart attack.


4. Major premise: Mommy says I'm stupid.
   Minor premise: Mommy is always right.
   Therefore: I'm stupid.

This is how negative concepts are programmed into the subconscious mind, and Spirit has no choice but to carry them out, no matter how harmful they are. Because of the importance of this concept, I want to repeat that Spirit cannot reason upon your ideas, It has no ability to analyze or evaluate them, but can only accept your orders, constructive or destructive. Therefore, correct programming of the mind must begin at the conscious level.

Your personality is much like a highly sophisticated computer. The soul is the programmer and must program data into the subconscious before it can receive output. In order for the deductive process to start, the subconscious must be given input in the form of premises, which are the data received from the soul. These premises are ideas that you originate yourself, or ones that you accept from others, such as your parents, teachers, clergy, mate, and advertisers in print and broadcast media. If, therefore, your life is a mess, *you* ordered it! Either you programmed your subconscious with negative orders, or you allowed someone else to do it for you, and now it is manifesting in your life. But, knowing how the personality functions, you can reverse the process and reprogram your subconscious mind to the positive ideas that will make your life happy and fulfilling!

You may be wondering how Spirit, which cannot reason or originate ideas, can give you direction and guide your life. You must ask It for help first; you have to tune into It, and then It will respond. Spirit doesn't need to originate answers for you; It already has all the answers in waiting. It selects the appropriate one, when you are ready and know how to ask for it, and presents it to you in the form of intuitive insights, visions or dreams.

Understanding how the mind functions, we must be very careful about what ideas we allow to become lodged in our subconscious. If you are wise, you will learn to keep eternal vigil over your soul in order to reject the myriad negative ideas with which we are all constantly bombarded. And, if you now have a number of negative concepts lodged in your subconscious which are dominating your life, you will find that the techniques for transformation covered in the remaining chapters of this book will help you to dislodge them. You have the power within you right now to reverse those ideas and create for yourself whatever type of life you want!

**part two**

# TECHNIQUES
# FOR
# TRANSFORMATION

# four
## SELF-HYPNOSIS: THE MAGIC DOORWAY

*The Cure of the Soul*
*Has to be Effected*
*by the Use of Certain Charms...*
*and These Charms are Fair Words.*
*—Socrates*

One of the fastest ways to tap the great powers of your subconscious mind is through self-hypnosis, which is a doorway to the tremendous storehouse of wisdom residing in your subconscious. There is no power in the world as great as the forces residing in your own mind, and self-hypnosis is a direct pipeline whereby you can release these powers. He or she who learns the technique of self-hypnosis has discovered the secret of successful living, thus it is important that you have a general understanding of the art of hypnosis in order to use self-hypnosis most effectively.

Many people still have some very confused notions about hypnosis because of the classic fictional portrait of a bearded Svengali with his long black cape, making weird passes over the helpless Trilby. And, unfortunately, it is true that some stage hypnotists have perverted the purpose of hypnosis by using it to make people bark like dogs and cluck like chickens and, in general, make fools of themselves. Occasionally, amateurs, after learning a few basic principles of hypnosis, use it to show off at parties and may cause harm by giving their subjects detrimental suggestions.

The danger is not in hypnosis per se, but in the application of it. Hypnosis is extremely beneficial because it is a state of very deep relaxation. In the hands of a trained professional, hypnosis can alleviate insomnia, cure impotence and other sexual dysfunctions, reduce anxiety, facilitate the overcoming of bad habits, and help our lives in a great many ways. Hypnosis has an essential place in psychotherapy, where it can be used to enhance the therapeutic process, and in surgery and dentistry, where it is used for the relief of pain.

Hypnosis doesn't necessarily mean that someone has to be in a trance, as the average person thinks of a trance state. It is merely an extension of common states of mind, of the everyday trances all of us have from time to time when we become deeply absorbed in reverie or preoccupied with something, oblivious as to what is happening around us.

We see waking hypnosis around us every day. It is not some strange, mysterious thing limited to abnormal conditions, but a daily occurrence for all of us. In its most elementary form it is called salesmanship. In its most profound form it can save your life. Have you ever been driving your car down the freeway and passed right by the exit where you wanted to get off? That's because you were in a mild hypnotic trance, deeply absorbed in thought. Or, have you ever driven through a town and later didn't remember having gone through it? That's hypnotic amnesia. We drive both consciously and subconsciously. It has become such a habit that the conscious mind can be totally engaged in talking or thinking while the subconscious keeps the car on the road. Typists are familiar with this phenomenon. One can be typing material while his or her mind is engaged in thinking of several different things because it is partly done unconsciously.

Hypnosis is simply a state of heightened suggestibility, and we are hypnotized any time we accept a suggestion from someone else. And it doesn't necessarily involve closing your eyes and going into a trance. Any time you accept the suggestion of another, that's a form of hypnosis. For instance, if I say, "you should wear your raincoat today because I think it's going to rain", and you do it, that's a form of mild hypnosis.

The ability to be hypnotized is not some mysterious, magical thing; it's really very easy and simple, and anyone can achieve it who is willing to try. Human life could not go on without the use of hypnosis because, if no one ever accepted a suggestion from someone else, nothing would happen. Business corporations pay huge fees to people who know the art of getting others to accept suggestions. Television commercials are filled with ideas which flow in such rapid succession and in so many attractive forms that observers do not have the opportunity to use their reason; thus, the suggestions are lodged in the subconscious mind. Whenever you go out and buy a product you have seen advertised on television, you are hypnotized to that extent. Life would be very limited without the power of suggestion, but it is a matter of learning to accept the right suggestions—the ideas that we want to see manifested in our lives, and also dehypnotizing ourselves to the negative suggestions we have already accepted.

Contrary to popular belief, no one can hypnotize you if you are unwilling; in the final analysis, all hypnosis is self-hypnosis. No one has any special power that you do not possess yourself. A hypnotist is merely a person who has learned a technique for helping you to contact your own subconscious mind. But, you must be willing to go along with the suggestions, or they won't work. If you are willing to play the part of the subject and allow someone else to play the part of the operator, you can be hypnotized. Hypnosis is a matter of degree; some people make excellent subjects right from the beginning and can go very deeply into the trance state, but others may require some training. Hypnosis is a learned ability; if you wish to become a good subject, you can be trained to respond at a deep level. The important thing to remember is that *the power to be hypnotized does not lie with the hypnotist, it lies with the subject.*

Hypnosis is imagination, not will power; it is not a matter of domination, or being weak-willed. This false idea has been perpetuated by stage hypnotists using such phrases as, "you're under my spell," or "you will do my bidding and are powerless to resist." This is sheer nonsense. Hypnosis is a matter of concentration and the willingness to accept suggestions, and has nothing whatsoever to do with will power. Highly intelligent, creative people, in fact, tend to be the best hypnotic subjects. Doctors Ernest and Josephine Hilgard, in the Psychology Department at Stanford University, discovered through research that university students who have a history of, and a capability for, a high degree of imaginative involvement, make excellent subjects. "By imaginative involvement," say the Hilgards, "is meant an absorption in some kind of fantasy so real that ordinary reality is set aside; the experience is felt as actually being lived, and is savored as such. The scientist who enjoys science fiction, without any detriment to his career as a critical scientist, furnishes an illustration of this flexibility. The areas of involvement differ from person to person—reading, music, religion, an aesthetic interest in nature, extensive daydreaming, some forms of physical activity, such as skiing, skin-diving, cave-exploring,—any of these areas may provide a preparation for and a path into hypnotic experience." Most people find self-hypnosis relatively easy to master, but others require more practice. It may be helpful for you to be put into a hypnotic trance by a professional person first because, once the state has been experienced, it is easier to do it yourself.

Although people fear giving up control to another person, the fact is that hypnosis will not rob you of your will power nor diminish your self-control. No one can force you to be hypnotized, nor can he or she make you do something under hypnosis that you don't want to do. If you are told to do something that is objectionable to you, you will simply sit and do nothing, or you will open your eyes and come out of the trance. I once told a man under hypnosis that the glass of water I handed him was Coca Cola. His eyes remained closed, but he would not take a sip of water. It turned out that he was a member of a church which did not allow drinking any beverage containing caffeine.

There is something operating within us that protects us from acting on suggestions that are contrary to our nature; otherwise, we would buy every product that advertisers pitch on television. Even so, you should never allow yourself to be hypnotized by a person who does not fully understand the incredible forces that are being dealt with under hypnosis. If you seek help for an emotional problem, carefully check the background and credentials of the hypnotist, who should be someone licensed in the healing arts, such as a psychologist, psychiatrist, marriage and family counselor, (certified in some states, such as California, to practice hypnosis), or clinical social worker.

Under hypnosis you will feel totally relaxed, calm, and peaceful; thus, the state of hypnosis is extremely beneficial to your body. And, hypnosis will help you get in touch with the profoundest part of your nature, the subconscious mind.

Contrary to popular belief, there is no loss of consciousness in hypnosis; the subject is actually acutely aware, even in the deepest stages. If the demonstration is before a group, the subject is conscious of the fact that he or she is being observed. During a class demonstration, I was once placed in a state of catalepsy by a hypnotist in order to be suspended in a horizontal position between two chairs, my body supported only by my head and feet. I had just had my hair styled that morning, and one of the men who lifted my rigid body into position accidently knocked my head and ruined my hair style. I was wholly aware of this, and was a little disturbed by it, but it didn't interfere with the trance.

It is entirely possible for a person to go into a trance with his or her eyes wide open and for the eyes to remain open all during the trance. And it is certainly possible to talk, although the speech is usually slowed down.

It is often difficult for most people to tell when they have achieved the hypnotic stage. The transition from the conscious to the trance state is so gradual, and the psychological and physiological evidence of change so subtle, it is practically impossible, especially when using self-hypnosis, to determine which state exists at any given moment. Some individuals experience feelings in hypnosis such as sensations of floating, disassociation from their bodies, lightheadedness, tingling, heaviness of the limbs, and so forth; but others notice very little difference. For example, I have hynotized people to stop smoking who felt nothing had actually taken place during the session, and the hypnosis hadn't worked, but who never smoked another cigarette again.

Another myth is that a hypnotized person is asleep. Although the induction procedure usually contains such suggestions as "you are feeling very sleepy and tired," what the subject achieves is a "sleep-resembling" state, but not actual sleep. The subject has to be sufficiently awake to hear the instructions of the hypnotist and, if he or she actually falls asleep, the instructions will not be carried out. Actually, although the muscles are loose and relaxed during hypnosis, the brain is acutely concentrated, and the subject is focused in on what the hypnotist is saying to a very high degree. Occasionally, a subject will go into a light sleep under hypnosis, and studies have shown that it is still effective because the suggestions of the hypnotist will go directly into the subconscious mind of the subject. If imagery work is being used, however, such as having an overweight woman imagine herself slim, it is better for the subject to be awake in order to participate in the visualization.

Another misconception about hypnosis is that there is a complete loss of memory for everything that has occurred. This happens very infrequently and usually only when the hypnotist has given the subject the direct suggestion that there will be amnesia regarding what has taken place. Under ordinary circumstances, a subject is aware of everything that is said, and able to remember it.

One of the great fears of many people is that they will reveal all their deep, dark secrets under hypnosis. Since hypnotic subjects are completely aware of their surroundings, they would no more betray a confidence, or embarrass themselves, than if they were wide awake in front of the same people. Subjects do not volunteer information under hypnosis; if a question should prove embarassing, they will simply sit there and say nothing. An alert hypnotist will spot the resistance and change the suggestion.

And what happens if the hypnotist dies, or walks away and never comes back while a subject is under hypnosis? Though this is extremely unlikely, all that will occur is that the subject will awaken spontaneously when ready. Very infrequently, a subject will not open his or her eyes when instructed to do so by the hypnotist. This is no cause for alarm; usually the person is simply tired and enjoying the rest. Given the suggestion that five minutes of hypnotic "sleep" is equal to five hours of real sleep, the person will awaken completely refreshed after five minutes elapse. Or, the subject can simply be allowed to awaken whenever he or she wants. In self-hypnosis, you will give yourself a pre-arranged signal to awaken at a certain time or after counting to a certain number.

The secret involved in hypnosis, including self-hypnosis, is an inner agreement with one's self. You must consciously cooperate in the process and be as open and receptive as possible. If you are thinking, "this isn't going to work," you lessen the efficacy of the process. If, on the other hand, you completely accept that you are going to be successful, your subconscious mind will accept it also. Affirming to yourself that what is being suggested is really happening leads to conviction.

A trained hypnotist is able to determine how deeply hypnotized a subject is by observing the bodily signs carefully or by making certain tests, such as locking the subject's fingers together or questioning him or her with prearranged finger signals.

Certain phenomena are characteristic of each of the three basic stages of hypnosis, although individual responses may vary.

**Lethargy** is the first and lightest stage of hypnosis and is characterized by muscular relaxation and dormancy of the senses.

The second stage is that of **Catalepsy.** It is usually produced by a sharp clap of the hands or another kind of loud noise in the ears of the lethargic subject. In this state the subject is characterized by a statuesque immobility. The muscles are rigid, not relaxed, and will remain in the most difficult postures for hours without apparent fatigue.

**Somnambulism** is the deepest stage of hypnosis. This state results in an increased activity of the senses and is the stage in which the wonders of hypnosis manifest. In this stage people are able to produce phenomena which they could not possibly duplicate while in their normal, waking state. These are the phenomena of tremendous feats of memory, superstrength, enormous acuity in hearing, etc,, that are sometimes reported in the news media. For example, you may have read in the newspapers a few years ago about the 110-pound mother who lifted a Volkwagen with one hand and pulled her trapped son from beneath it with the other. Under normal conditions she would have been incapable of this kind of strength, but at that moment of panic her rational mind was not operating to tell her she was not capable of lifting a car, so she tapped directly into her subconscious mind and found the ability inherent within her. This was a state of self-induced hypnosis. And this is what hypnosis demonstrates: that there are virtually limitless capabilities within all of us if we only learn how to tap the wisdom of the subconscious mind.

The reason hypnosis works is because of the following four principles:

1. **Imagination is more powerful than will power.**

In any battle between the will and the imagination, the imagination always wins. If you imagine something under hypnosis, even though your reason is telling you it isn't so, you will produce the effect through imagination. Using this principle, you should employ your imagination, not your reason, if you want to achieve something. For instance, if you want to lose a few pounds and are offered a delicious-looking dish of ice cream, you should immediately imagine how attractive and happy you will be when you reach your weight goal, rather than trying to use will power to argue against accepting the dessert. If, instead, you begin to imagine how good the ice cream will taste, and then attempt to use your will power to resist the temptation, you will be defeated.

2. **Imagination is more powerful than reason.**

This principle has led many normal, rational people to follow blindly a rabble-rouser or a Hitler because their imagination overpowered their reason. This is also why the con artist is successful: he manipulates people's imagination. And it is also why we sometimes fall in love with someone whom our reason tells us is totally wrong for us, but something about them has captured our imagination (our fantasy), and we are overcome by it. Creative people, who have highly developed imaginations, are excellent subjects for hypnosis. Youngsters are also very responsive to hypnosis because their imagination is less restrained and rigid than that of their elders.

3. **Only one idea can be entertained by the mind at any one given time.**

If a hypnotist tells you that your hands are stuck tightly together, either you must affirm to yourself that they are, or say "no, they are not." Conflicting ideas cannot be held at one and the same time thus, to be successful in hypnosis, you must not resist the suggestion given.

4. **Any imagined condition will become real if persisted in, provided only that it is logical.**

The subconscious mind cannot tell the difference between an idea which is strongly imagined and something that is actually happening in the outer world. That is why hypnosis and imaging work. After a period of incubation of the hypnotic suggestion, it will begin to manifest itself in your life.

## Inducing Self-Hypnosis

The first requirement for inducing self-hypnosis, is to get into a relaxed position. Sit in a comfortable chair, hands loosely on your lap, legs uncrossed and feet flat on the floor. Focus your eyes on a point near the ceiling. Almost any object of eye fixation will do, but be sure it is above eye level since this puts a small strain on the eyes and makes it easier to close them. As you focus on this object, say to yourself: "My eyelids are becoming heavier and heavier. Soon they will be so heavy that they will close. Soon I will be totally relaxed." Pay close attention to your eyelids; as you repeat the sentences to yourself, you will feel the desire to close your eyes. Don't resist the urge, just allow your eyes to close when you are ready.

As an alternative, you can count from one to ten, closing your eyes on the even numbers and opening them on the odd ones. Your eyes should stay closed by the time you get to ten; if not, simply begin your count again.

As your eyes close, it is a good idea to use a key phrase, such as "relax now," to deepen the state. This phrase should be repeated very slowly three times. This will become your trigger for inducing the state again and should be used each time. If you wish you can use the "Relaxation Concept" in Appendix A to bring your entire body into a state of deep relaxation after you close your eyes.

The next step is to choose a way to induce increased, deep muscular relaxation. A common image used by hypnotists is the suggestion of going down in an elevator, while counting the floors from one to ten. If you are afraid of elevators, you can use an escalator or staircase. I usually find, however, that by giving the suggestion to subjects that "this is a very safe elevator, perfectly safe in every way," even those who dislike elevators are not averse to riding it in their imagination. You can count from floors one to ten, or backwards from ten to one, just as though you were going down into the basement of a large department store. The idea of going *down* into the subconscious is a symbol which is universally used; going *up* symbolizes the conscious mind. Going down is, of course, associated with going deeper.

As you begin your slow descent and accompanying count of the floors you pass, repeat phrases to yourself which indicate relaxing, getting sleepy and tired, going deeper and deeper. In your mind's eye, see the numbers on the elevator indicator taking you further and further down.

When you arrive at the bottom floor, imagine the elevator door opening to a room that has a big, soft, comfortable bed in it. You walk over to the bed, stretch out on it, and go into an hypnotic sleep. As you lie down on the bed, say to yourself:   I am now in a very pleasant hypnotic sleep, and I will stay in this state until I come back up the elevator.   (Or, until you count to ten, or whatever prearranged signal you decide on.)

You will now be at least lightly in hypnosis and, after practice, will be able to achieve a deep state. If you feel that you are not completely relaxed while lying in the bed, imagine some other scene of relaxation—lying on the grass under a tree on a warm, summer day, or sitting by a placid lake, or even relaxing in a hot bath. Use any image that conveys to you the idea of becoming more deeply relaxed.

While you are in a state of hypnosis, time may seem to pass very quickly. Sometimes it seems as though you have been in the state for an hour or so although it's actually only been fifteen minutes. You may even drop off into a light sleep if you are tired. You can avoid this by taking a sitting, not reclining, position and by giving yourself suggestions that you will remain awake. It is crucial to be awake in self-hypnosis because you have to give yourself suggestions. You can also give yourself a post-hypnotic suggestion that you will awaken fully at a specific time so that you control the length of time you remain under. This is the technique many people use who are able to nap for exactly one hour and always wake up at the designated time.

In your initial sessions you must allow yourself at least a half hour for induction and suggestions. After you become proficient at self-hypnosis, you should be able to put yourself under in as little as five minutes, then take another ten minutes or so for your suggestions.

After you have given yourself the suggestion that you are now in a hypnotic sleep, test to see the depth of your state of hypnosis, and practice accepting a suggestion you make to yourself.

A good initial test is the "stuck eyelids test." With your eyes closed, say to yourself: "I am going to count to five; at the count of five, my eyelids will be stuck tightly together, and I will be unable to open them until I am ready to wake up."
Then repeat something like the following:
1.    My eyelids are now sticking tightly together, and I will be unable to open them.
2.    The harder I try, the tighter the lids will stick together.
3.    My eyelids are now stuck tightly together, just as though there were a thick, heavy glue on them locking them together; and I cannot open my eyes.
4.    In a moment I am going to try to open my eyelids, but I will not be able to do so because they are locked so tightly together. It is impossible to open them; the harder I try, the more they resist.
5.    Tight, tight, locked tight; and I cannot open my eyes until I am ready to wake up.
Now, try to open your eyes. If the test is successful, you eyelids will stay closed no matter how hard you try to open them. The

43

principle involved here is that you cannot think two conflicting thoughts at the same time. As long as you strongly believe that you cannot open your eyes, it will be quite impossible to open them. In accepting your suggestion, your subconscious blocks the nerve impulses from reaching the muscles of your eyelids, so they will not move.

Some people may not like to use this test since the thought of not being able to open their eyes is frightening,even though they're in control. If you feel this way, use a similar test, the "hand-clasp test." Before entering hypnosis, interlock your fingers in a comfortable position in your lap. After the induction process, give yourself the same type of suggestions which are used for stuck eyelids, but substitute stuck hands. As you lock your hands together, squeeze the palms tightly and visualize a thick, heavy glue locking them in this position. Either of these tests will deepen hypnosis.

If you fail the test, give yourself further suggestions to deepen the relaxation, such as: "As I lie here relaxing, I am going deeper and deeper and becoming more and more relaxed. Every muscle, nerve, and fibre of my body is now deeply relaxed. Physical comfort exists, and my subconscious mind has slowed down my breathing and pulse rate as I relax even deeper. I am becoming an excellent hypnotic subject, and my subconscious mind is responding to all my suggestions. Now I am drifting down more and more rapidly and becoming more drowsy and tired. I am now going into a very pleasant hypnotic sleep."

You can also use a hand signal, such as saying to yourself: "When my index finger rises, I will then be in a deep hypnotic trance." Then wait for your subconscious mind to carry out this order.

Once you are in a hypnotic state, tell yourself: "My subconscious mind is now totally open and receptive to everything I am saying. It will carry out all of my instructions because this is what I consciously desire." At this point you should begin giving yourself direct, positive suggestions for whatever it is that you wish. In Appendix B, which includes a sample induction talk, there are suggestions you can use to stop smoking, lose weight, or gain more self-confidence. These samples can be used as a guide for constructing suggestions for whatever it is that you want to work on through self-hypnosis.

It's a good idea to write out your suggestions in advance so that they are exact. You must be very careful not to program your subconscious mind with incorrect suggestions. A beginner should always carefully edit his or her ideas and follow the rules outlined in

44

Chapter 6 on visualization. Suggestions can be abbreviated into a key word, such as "healthy," "slender," or "confident" when you are in a hurry and don't have sufficient time for the entire program. Or, you can condense the idea into one sentence, such as "I am now rapidly losing weight."

Repetition is the main rule in giving effective suggestions. Repeat your suggestions at least three times to be sure that they penetrate into your subconscious mind. Certainly, advertisers are aware of this principle; television commercials are repeated over and over again so that the conscious mind becomes bored with them and ceases to pay attention. At that point the commercial goes directly into the subconscious without hindrance.

Mental imagery should be added to your positive suggestions, because the subconscious thinks in pictures. The technique of visualization is discussed fully in Chapter 6; suffice to say that you should, in your mind's eye, *see* yourself being slender, acting confidently, passing an exam, or whatever you are working on. The visual image should always represent the desired result. It's best to work on no more than two suggestions at one time so that your energy doesn't become scattered over too wide a field. Or, you can work on one objective for a week and then switch to another while your subconscious mind begins carrying out the first suggestions.

When you are ready to awaken from your hypnotic state, say to yourself: "I will easily be able to carry out all the suggestions I have given myself. The next time I do this, I will be able to go even deeper, very quickly. I will now count from one to five (or whatever your prearranged awakening signal is). At the count of five, I will awaken, completely refreshed and rejuvenated, full of energy, and feeling wonderful in every way!"

To summarize the main points in this chapter:

1.     Write out your suggestions so that they are accurate and exact.

2.     Symbolize the suggestions with a key word (conditioned response).

3.     Read your suggestions aloud before hypnotizing yourself to set them in your mind.

4.     Select a quiet place where you can spend an uninterrupted fifteen to thirty minutes each day practicing self-hypnosis.

5.     Seat yourself in a comfortable chair with your hands resting in your lap and your legs uncrossed.

6.     Fix your eyes on a spot above eye level. As you are staring at this spot, relax your body and tell yourself repeatedly that your eyelids are getting very, very heavy and that they will soon close and

stay closed until you are ready to come out of the hypnotic state.

7. With your eyes closed, talk to yourself about becoming more relaxed. Start at the top of your head and relax every muscle down to your feet, or work in a reverse pattern. Begin with your key phrase, "relax now."

8. Visualize a restful scene, such as lying down on the soft grass in the woods, taking a hot bath, going down in an elevator to the tenth floor, and stretching out in a comfortable bed.

9. Give yourself a triggering cue, such as raising your index finger to indicate to yourself that you are now in hypnosis. When this occurs, say to yourself, "I am now in deep hypnosis."

10. Visualize the outcome of your suggestion, using as much sensory input as possible. For example, visualize yourself at your desired weight and wearing clothes that will fit you at that size. Visualize other people telling you how good you look.

11. Give yourself direct, positive suggestions that you are now doing what you want to do and being what you want to become.

12. Work on only one, or at most two, suggestions within one session.

13. Before giving the signal to awaken, tell yourself that you will carry out all the suggestions you have made and that you will go even deeper into hypnosis the next time. Remind yourself that you will feel refreshed, rejuvenated, and energetic upon awakening.

14. Practice the art of self-hypnosis every day to become an adept practitioner.

This method of self-hypnosis, if applied diligently, will help you to achieve your desired goals in life. Excellent progress in self-development can be made by anyone who is willing to take the time to form a relationship with her subconscious mind. You have the power; all you need to do is apply it!

Hypnosis is the key to a happier life, and the means whereby we can contact our higher self. This Great Power within stands ready to serve our every need, if only we will call upon it. By means of this technique, you can set your goals and reach them, and learn how to gain information from your subconscious mind that you are not aware of consciously. In ancient Greece there was an inscription over the Temple of Delphos which simply stated: "Know Thyself." Hypnosis is a means whereby one can come into contact with the deepest part of oneself, and thereby live a much fuller life.

# THEORY OF HYPNOSIS

Ideas are conceived in the conscious part of the mind which turns them over to the subconscious, and the subconscious responds to the idea and begins carrying it out. The conscious mind produces the impression, while the subconscious produces the expression. It is always the conscious mind that determines what is to be done, and the subconscious furnishes the power with which to do it. You, the soul, have the ability to think the thought, to make the decision, to create an idea, but you do not have the power to carry it out. For example, if you wish to raise your hand to ask a question in a class, you can consciously make the decision, but you don't know how to move the muscles involved in that act. The subconscious does the work, and you know nothing about how it operates, all you can consciously do is originate the idea.

Under hypnosis, the conscious mind relinquishes for the time being its originative ability, and turns that over to the hypnotist. The hypnotist then temporarily becomes the originator for the individual, and thinks up the idea which the subconscious of the subject will carry out. Thus we form under hypnosis what may be termed a "composite personality" between two individuals, acting together as one.

Remember that the subconscious mind can function only deductively. This was explained in Chapter 3 on *Reprogramming the Mind*. It has absolutely no power to reason, analyze, judge, select, negate or disagree with any idea that is given it. Selection of ideas must be done at the conscious level because, once a concept is accepted by the conscious mind, it penetrates the subconscious and remains there permanently, regardless of whether it is true or false, right or wrong. The simple secret of lodging an idea into the subconscious is this: *If it's logical, it lodges; and if it lodges, you're hooked!* Now, logical does not necessarily mean *true*. It simply means that the idea cannot be refuted by the present knowledge of the conscious part of the mind, and thus it is accepted, sinks into the subconscious, and becomes a part of the psychic fabric of the person.

Since it cannot reject or negate ideas that are given it by the conscious mind, if you wish to tell your subconscious that this or that is harmful to you, and may cause you to eventually have a heart attack, or develop cancer, or whatever destructive idea you give it, it will simply begin carrying out your order. If you repeatedly tell your subconscious mind that you are inadequate, fearful, incompetent, unable to succeed financially, and so forth, it will accommodate you

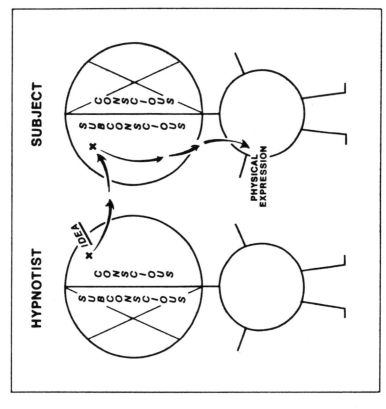

**COMPOSITE PERSONALITY OF HYPNOSIS**

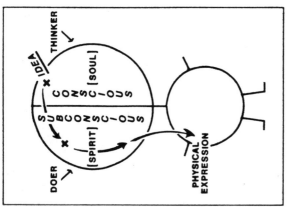

**ORDINARY OPERATION**

48

and obey your order. If the subconscious could reject certain ideas, and select only those which were for our health and growth, we would never be sick, we would never fail, and we would always be happy, healthy, competent individuals. But we would not have any free will. We would all be basically the same, because the subconscious would select only constructive, positive ideas, and reject the rest. This, however, is not the function of the subconscious mind. The soul (conscious mind) must be in charge of the personality, and it is the job of the soul to select the correct, positive, healthy ideas that it wants to see manifested in the person's life.

When a person is under hypnosis you are contacting directly the subconscious mind, and it will not argue with the ideas you give it. For example, if you should tell a person under hypnosis, when the subconscious is laid bare, that she has superstrength, or will not feel any pain when you put a needle in her arm, Spirit will not question it, and will carry out the suggestion. The one function of the subconscious is to express the ideas that it has been given, and it never objects nor reasons upon what is said, but willingly accepts and obeys.

Ideas which get into the subconscious can come either from other persons, or they may originate in the individual's own conscious mind. The important thing to remember is that ideas or concepts are lodged in every person's subconscious and, if they are of a negative character, they will sooner or later cause trouble in the individual's physical and emotional life. The subconscious mind is the power behind the throne; it is the source of dynamic energy in a person's life. It receives the impressions of the thoughts and desires of the conscious mind, and expresses them inevitably in the physical organism, and in the character and life of the person. The subconscious is the great inner world from which all things proceed. What is programmed *there* is what governs our lives!

Dr. Fleet, founder of Concept-Therapy says: "To an extent greater than you have ever dreamed, you get from life exactly what you expect innately. Your subconscious power arranges your affairs and draws to you exactly those things and conditions which you have thought about and visualized in your conscious thinking. What you are now, your position in life, is the result of past thought. There is no such thing as chance. You have visualized a certain mode of life and thought about it to such an extent that you have directed your subconscious power to manifest it for you." Thus, if you want to know what you've been asking for, look at what you've got. If you don't like it, you have the power to change it, by the very same process through which it originally became manifest.

49

Remember, the great Innate Power does not think. It has no power to reason; It cannot of Itself act, but must be set in motion either from your own thought, or from an impression gained from others. The Techniques for Transformation presented in this book show how you may consciously direct Spirit properly, so that you can change your whole life for the better. Not only can you change your environment, or your financial condition, you can even alter the state of your physical and mental health. Remember always that the subconscious is your servant. You are the originator of ideas, and all that is required is for you to conceive positive ideas, instead of those which are negative. By holding these concepts in their mind constantly, they will gradually sink down into your subconscious, and then will begin to manifest in your life. You therefore become a creator in your own right, and create positive thoughts which will in time be brought into manifestation.

So far as we know this Innate Power is limitless. What you really desire and confidently expect you will receive. Therefore, use this Great Power intelligently. Think positive, constructive thoughts, and never entertain negative, destructive ideas! If you desire something in your life which is constructive and which it is proper for you to have, then visualize that something, and you will find that in time it will come to you. There must be a series of mental pictures adapted to the end you have in mind. There must be daily repetition of the mental picture or the suggestion and, if this is persisted in without entertaining any doubts as to its eventual manifestation, that something will surely come to you. Your only limitations are your own thoughts—you have no other limitations!

# five

# DEVELOPING YOUR INTUITION

*You ask me where I get my ideas,*
*That I cannot tell you with certainty;*
*They come unsummoned, directly, indirectly—*
*I could seize them with my hands—*
*out in the open air;*
*in the woods, while walking;*
*in the silence of the night;*
*early in the morning*
*incited by moods,*
*which are translated by the poet*
*into words,*
*by me, into tones*
*that sound and roar and storm about me*
*until I have set them down in notes.*
*—Ludwig Von Beethoven*

Although this book presents a variety of methods for achieving success in life, it must be remembered that true happiness does not come from material possessions, prestige, power or status. Many who have gained all of these things have been very lonely, troubled individuals. Deep and lasting fulfillment can come only from developing an harmonious relationship with your inner self. The first step, always, is to work at becoming the person you want to be; then the things you want to have in your life will follow automatically.

We live on four planes: the physical, mental, emotional, and spiritual, and all of these aspects of our existence must be nurtured and cared for if we are to become completely healthy, self-actualizing human beings. The needs for meaning, for higher values, for a spiritual life, are as real as biological and social needs. Two great psychiatrists, Roberto Assagioli, author of *Psychosynthesis*, and Carl Jung, strongly stressed the need to develop our higher psychic functions, the spiritual dimension of our lives, since this awareness leads to a feeling of wholeness, security, and joy.

It seems that what we are experiencing in this technological age is an impoverishment of our spiritual selves. We are living in a society surfeiting us with "things" that we are constantly urged to purchase, yet offering us little to nourish the higher, aesthetic side of our nature; so the inner self is often parched and neglected. We have some evidence of this in the enormous number of neurotic and unhappy people we see around us, many of whom are consuming a tremendous quantity of prescription and non-prescription drugs, alcohol, and other substances to mitigate their psychic pain. We have to realize, and often life forces us to realize, that the spiritual aspect of our personality must be nourished, and is as vital to our lives as food and water. "To not give credence to the spiritual life," physicist Albert Einstein once stated, "is to deny the validity of human experience."

It is really not possible to live an emotionally healthy life without making some contact with our inner self. We can develop ourselves intellectually, emotionally, or in our career, but eventually we must satisfactorily answer the deepest, most fundamental questions of life if we are to actualize our full potential as human beings; the most advanced creatures on earth. Questions such as, "what is the meaning of my life?" and, "what is my purpose and ultimate goal?" are basic to living a joyous, harmonious life, yet they are the very questions which our academic institutions largely ignore. Thus, our schools and universities are graduating students who know how to program computers and analyze data, but who know very little about how to live a life constructively and gain the greatest fulfillment from it.

We are all aware that we have five outer senses—hearing, seeing, smelling, tasting, and touching—that bring us information about the external world. But we are often unaware that we also have inner senses, such as intuition, imagination, perception, clairvoyance, and other faculties which can be categorized as extrasensory perception. Civilized man has chosen to ignore these inner senses, so they have become diminished through neglect. Yet, there is a wealth of hidden knowledge within the subconscious realm of our minds, to which we could avail ourselves if we would only listen. All of our faculties can be consciously developed, stimulated, and augmented because they are in a state of *becoming*, either developing or diminishing as we grow older, depending upon the amount of attention we give to them.

In order to expand our consciousness and begin to live in a higher dimension, we must develop these intuitive faculties, and they will start to open up by a natural process when we consciously attempt to live a higher life and express the positive emotions, such as love, joy, and compassion. Though many people today have a smattering of extrasensory capacity, most have not developed their spiritual consciousness in the slightest. Unfortunately, some of these so-called psychic people are even misusing their gift as an ego trip by pretending they have something that others don't. I cannot emphasize strongly enough that this gift of intuitive power is available to all of us when we are open to receive it.

One of the most fundamental and necessary methods of developing and expanding the higher faculties is meditation, the single most important pathway to higher consciousness. Through constant and persistent meditation, the voice of intuition speaks to us to guide and help our lives.

So often people avoid meditation, claiming it is too difficult to learn the correct method. Is there a correct method? Is it necessary to take courses in specific techniques and learn intricate disciplines before you can meditate in the most appropriate way? I can only answer those questions by echoing the great Indian teacher Krishnamurti: "Do not ask me how to meditate, do it!" Meditation can begin with the simplest of thoughts: "Who am I?" And then listen to the thoughts that follow. Or this: "I am an expression of the Infinite. How has Spirit chosen to express Itself through me?"

When meditation becomes habitual, a permanent change takes place in one's life, and one begins to perceive the existence of something beyond the five senses. As you become more spiritually-minded, you will realize that the inner strength you can build during meditation will help you to overcome any deficiency in your life. Every time you practice meditation, you make a gain which becomes a soul-possession and a soul-profit forevermore.

History records that the most highly evolved lights of this world—Socrates, Plato, Walt Whitman, Mary Baker Eddy, and so forth—all spent a great deal of time contemplating inwardly, getting in touch with their higher nature, which is the only way to self-realization. These great souls were, for the most part, solitary individuals; men and women who walked alone, thought alone, and communed with nature alone. In solitude each came to grips with the meaning of his or her life and the direction it should be channeled. It is in these moments of solitude that we can discover our inner self, and realize the true nature of our relationship with life.

Most people run away from the challenge of being with themselves by attempting to find themselves through someone else. People who are afraid to be left in isolation with themselves surround their lives with constant noise and distractions, thereby drowning out the still, small voice within. If, instead of running away, you will learn to spend time with yourself, you will have the joyous experience of discovering who you really are on the deepest levels of your being.

It is not necessary to turn away from the world by hiding in a monastery or Himalayan cave in order to achieve this attitude. One can learn to remain in the midst of conflict and confront it for what it is, yet maintain their serenity. Real happiness comes from struggling with the difficult and overcoming it, not avoiding it. People who live what may be called the contemplative life, or the spiritual life, do not allow their inner peace to be disturbed by all the confusion and dissonance of the outer world; and that's what makes their lives different. To make room for a deeper understanding, the ego has to be moved over; and the only way to do this is to have sufficient time and silence to allow Spirit the opportunity to speak to your mind and heart. Unless we make some room in our consciousness for Spirit to incline us from within, we cannot hear Its guiding voice. Meditation, then, is not a withdrawal from the world; it is a return to reality, but it's a different view of reality.

Meditation is a formidable *Technique for Transformation* and requires no elaborate preparation, so you can begin using this technique right now even before you finish reading this book. To assist you, here are some simple steps that will create the appropriate mood.

Fundamental to successful meditation is a quiet place with no distractions. Plan to meditate fifteen minutes to a half hour when you begin. Later, as you start to experience the benefits accrued from this quiet time, you may wish to extend it. Be sure you will not be disturbed by the telephone, the kids, or the dog for, if you are concerned about interruptions, it will interfere with your achieving maximum introspection. It will be especially helpful if you have a separate room you can use at this time; if not, reserve a special chair for use only when you are meditating. This helps trigger a "conditioned reflex" whenever you sit in that chair, which is conducive to your intention. It is best to meditate with the lights out and your eyes closed. If this bothers you, however, simply dim the lights so that they will not be distracting. Begin your meditation by relaxing your body as much as possible. If you wish, you can use the relaxation formula given in Apppendix A to accomplish this.

When you first begin to meditate, it will probably require a week or two to train your mind to focus on the task at hand. The mind is a great trickster and often brings up things you would least like to think about at the beginning of meditation! If you are already accustomed to meditating but have ceased practicing it for a period of time, you will probably find that it takes a week or two to get back in tune with it. Have patience, whether you are a novice or a former practitioner, for the rewards are great!

I like to divide my meditation period into two parts, one which I call concentration, and the other "decentration", or the active and passive parts of my session. In the active part, after calming my body and mind, I spend five to ten minutes making visual images and affirmations for things I want to achieve in my life. Procedures for doing this are described in later chapters.

When I feel this is complete, I begin the passive part of my meditation, during which the inspirational thoughts and deeper effects occur. This is the time when you attempt to move your ego-self out of the way to listen quietly to your inner voice. At this stage, you must shut down the machinery of your mind as much as possible and simply allow thoughts, flashes of intuition, and guidance from Spirit to come to you. Occasionally, this can be a time of sublime joy, a time when you make contact with the Infinite and feel a peaceful, blissful unity with all life. This is the ecstasy spoken of by mystics and saints and, though rare, is the greatest benefit of meditation and its highest achievement. And it is available to anyone willing to put in the necessary time and effort.

To achieve this state, you need a method for stilling the numerous thoughts of the mind. The best way of doing this is either to concentrate on your breathing or choose a "mantra," a single, meaningless sound on which to focus. Transcendental Meditation masters give students a particular Sanskrit word upon which they concentrate to clear the mind; but, Dr. Herbert Benson, author of *The Relaxation Response,* found that the word "One" is equally effective.

Personally, I have found that concentrating on slowing down my breathing as much as possible, accomplishes the same objective. One way of doing this is to breathe in slowly to the count of eight, hold your breath for a count of eight, then breathe out slowly to the count of eight. There must be no strain whatsoever in doing this; so if eight counts are difficult for you to hold, try a smaller count until you feel comfortable. Continue doing this until your body feels almost motionless and your mind is equally stilled. When this occurs, a feeling of peace, harmony and oneness will often flood your being. Sometimes intuitive insights and messages from the subconscious will accompany this.

The most effective way to achieve self-mastery is through meditation. The inner strength you gain will help you overcome any lack in your life, and you will find the time of peaceful meditation not only inspiring but of great benefit to your physical and emotional well-being. Researchers have demonstrated that meditation can reduce hypertension, eliminate headaches, and alleviate a variety of other medical problems.

The contemplative person, states Thomas Merton, in his *Seven Story Mountain,* "ceases to identify himself with the actions that are contributing to the problems, to the violence, the madness of the mob. He watches the play but he is not emotionally involved in it. Yet at the same time he is not under the delusion that he is better than those who are involved in it. It is not the world that is bad, but the way of being in the world which kills that which is most vital in man if he becomes enslaved to it. And then one experiences within oneself the entrapment of the Spirit, or the separation of the lower nature from the higher...and the person has lost himself. One who is free from the controlling domination of his emotions is the only one who can think intelligently. Since he is not governed solely by his passions, he can see clearly, and thus he acts clearly from this standpoint of self-mastery."

Through regular meditation you come continuously closer to alignment of the self with the Infinite Wisdom and Power. And through meditation you can achieve a greater sense of the spiritual and cosmic nature of your life by turning your consciousness to your Higher Self Within. It is invaluable to the evolution of your consciousness and, in fact, is the only way to discover the Real Self Within and reawaken that within you which is eternal. Once you are in contact with your higher mind, anything is possible to you. The pathway to love, security, and inner peace is reached by integrating all the aspects of yourself: spiritual, mental, emotional, and physical. Make continuous efforts to contact Spirit Within, thus awakening your higher self, which will guide and direct you in achieving your goals in life. This is a beautiful, noble, loving way to live, and it will bring you total fulfillment.

*The most beautiful and most profound emotion*
*we can experience is the sensation*
*of the mystical. It is the power of all*
*true science. ...To know that what is*
*impenetrable to us really exists, manifesting*
*itself as the highest wisdom and the most*
*radiant beauty which our dull faculties*
*can comprehend only in their most primitive*
*form—this knowledge, this feeling, is at*
*the center of true religiousness.*
*—Albert Einstein*

# six

# IMAGINATION:
# THE KEY TO THE KINGDOM

*Imagination is the beginning*
*of all creativity*
*You imagine what you desire,*
*You will what you imagine;*
*and at last*
*You create what you will.*
—*George Bernard Shaw*

All the great men and women in this world have used the power of imagination to create the successful lives they have achieved. These people have become great because they dared to imagine great achievement. They constantly pictured in their minds what they wanted, and the Power Within, given these pictures to work on, eventually brought them into being.

We are all directly or indirectly responsible for everything that happens to us even though it's often easier to blame someone else or some circumstance beyond our control. But, if we have knowledge of how the mind works, we will recognize that the way we think and feel has an intimate connection with what is happening to us.

If we get up in the morning thinking it's going to be a bad day with nothing going right, that's probably what will occur. Our thoughts go out into the universe in the form of vibrations and attract to us exactly what we are sending out. So, if you are always surrounded by difficulties, the solution is to change the pictures in your mind and image a more positive, fulfilling life.

Creative visualization is the technique of using your imagination in a systematic, structured way to create what you want. Of course, we all use our imagination constantly, usually in an unconscious, haphazard, or negative fashion. Worry, for example, is an extremely powerful image, and worried thoughts are always negative and destructive. Every time you fret about not getting the raise you want, or having a car accident, or not making your sales quota, you are programming your mind destructively. Since we have been taught so many negative concepts about ourselves, we automatically expect and *imagine* that we will have difficulties, limitation and misfortune. And thus we bring it into being.

Properly directed imagination is the key to the doorway to success, love, health, abundance, satisfying relationships, self-confidence, and greater self-expression. All we need do is become consciously aware of what we are creating and change the programming if we don't like it. Let us begin with an analysis of the type of suggestions many people have been given during the process of growing up.

Everyone has a basic concept about themselves which was formed mainly by the ideas others gave us in early life, and also by the feedback we receive from people today. Unfortunately, many people's basic concept of themselves includes ideas such as failure, rejection, inferiority, ill health, worthlessness, financial instability, and other destructive thoughts. Here are some typical basic concepts I frequently hear from my clients:

"I'm not capable of earning a good living."
"I feel inferior."
"I'm too sensitive, everything upsets me."
"I can't get good grades in school."
"I have a poor memory."
"I'll never be successfull."
"I'm not as smart as other people."
"I can't lose weight.
"I'm unloveable."

All of us have been exposed to negative ideas like these as we grew up. Do you remember your parents saying things like "you'll never amount to anything," "you can't do anything right," "you're really stupid," "you're so awkward and clumsy," "you're really not very bright," "you're lazy and selfish," "you're the pretty one, but Marsha's the intelligent one," or similar phrases? Or, maybe a teacher told you "you can't spell so you might as well forget it," "you'll never be able to do math," or "you just have a lousy memory." Statements such as these, though often intended to motivate, acutely impair our confidence and self-esteem. Constant reinforcement of such negative ideas may cause a person to feel socially inadequate and unable to communicate with others.

Some time ago I facilitated a therapy group in which a woman stated that her mother constantly told her: "Oh Mary, you just don't have any personality." And she didn't. This unfortunate woman was inhibited from developing her social skills, and her natural self-expression was thwarted by a dominant idea that she was inadequate.

If you feel this way, your self-concept is the cause of it all. We place our own limitations upon ourselves, and it's nothing more than an idea operating in the subconscious mind. Granted, many of these negative ideas were given to us by others when we were too young and too helpless to reject them. But now that we are adults, we can change these ideas and reprogram our minds by the same process. Whatever is occurring now in your life is the result of an image in your mind, and whatever will happen in the future will be the result of *your* images, not someone else's. All that is required is to make a correct image of that which you want to see happen in your life or personality, and turn that image over to the Creative Power Within to manifest it.

Your future is determined by the thoughts you think today! What you think you are—you are! And, you can become whatever you would like to be. In his wonderful book *The Crack in the Cosmic Egg* Joseph Chilton Pearce talks about the "statistical world," the so-called world of reality. Many people are fond of stating that they are "realistic," thus, they lock themselves into the statistical world, invariably bowing before the dictates of statistics and "facts," and accepting life on the basis of random chance.

We are constantly being programmed to statistics, such as: "So many people in this room will die of cancer this year," "Five hundred people will be killed on our highways this holiday weekend" Jobs these days are hard to get because the unemployment rate is at an all-time high". Of course these are facts. The statistical world is a reality because there are people who will make those statistics come true. They are people who have little control over their lives because they know nothing about the power of their own minds, and they are the helpless victims of life's vicissitudes. One who is able to think positively, however, and control his/her thoughts, need not be caught in the trap of statistics. Such a person can consciously be superior to the "Slings and arrows of outrageous fortune." As Pearce states, "An ultimately serious commitment of mind, combined with the active use of the imagination, can be the determining factor in any issue, overcoming all the odds against you, and overcoming chance.

In making images for the things you desire, you must be careful not to discuss them with people who cannot share your vision. A negative person can totally destroy your image by causing you to doubt its credibility. Holding an image of your desire takes a great deal of energy, especially when the odds are against your achieving it. You have to work hard enough at overcoming your own doubt without allowing others, who do not understand the power of the mind, to influence you. Pearce states that *nonambiguity is the shaping force of reality!* This is a tremendously important statement because it means that, when you remove all doubt that you will receive what you have imaged, it is sure to come to you. Believe in your images with all your strength, and don't allow nonbelievers to distort or destroy your faith by quoting statistics or telling you all the reasons why you cannot achieve them.

**Creativity and Imagination**

Creating what you want in life depends upon the use of the most potent force in the world: imagination, because, *by sustaining mental images of any kind, good or bad, you will eventually bring about a physical effect,* provided only that your images are logical. Unfortunately, our educational system stifles imagination by placing all the emphasis on rational thought. And that's one reason why our young people are so bored with shcool. If you have a child with an active imagination, you have a potential genius, for all creative people have highly developed imaginations. That is the source of their ideas, the realm of the inner life. Einstein stated that: "Imagination is more important than knowledge," adding that many of his ideas came to him while he was daydreaming or fantasizing, and not while he was applying his intellect to a problem.

Since creativity depends upon imagination—the ability to look at things in a different and imaginative way—then it follows that, if we wish to be more creative, we can do so by developing our imagination. Some people, such as artists, writers and musicians, appear to be born with a great imaginative ability, but this is a skill that can be learned by anyone. Sometimes in my seminars people will tell me that they simply cannot image any of the things I suggest during the processes. This is not really so; everyone can image things, but we all do this differently.Some people actually visualize an image projected before them when they close their eyes, but others merely "get a feeling" of the object, activity or event.

**Visualization and Psychotherapy**

One of the early pioneers of visualization, Dr. Joseph Wolpe, a psychiatrist at the University of Virginia School of Medicine, used imagery as a way to help people suffering from phobias. He believed that a phobia was a learned behavior, not a result of childhood trauma, and that the phobia could be "unlearned" if his patient could develop an opposing response to fear. He hit on the idea of teaching

60

phobic people to relax deeply in the presence of the desired object; after all, one cannot be afraid and relaxed at the same time. There was a drawback to the procedure, however, because it was sometimes not practical to be present with his patients when they faced the thing they feared, such as flying in a plane. Dr. Wolpe then experimented with having his patients *imagine* the phobic object while relaxed. It worked! In a few short sessions people were able to overcome phobias they'd had for years through this method, which psychologists call "systematic desensitization." Imagery is now widely used in modern psychotherapy and has proven to be extremely effective in helping clients handle life crises.

I once worked with a homemaker who had become so depressed that she had great difficulty getting up in the morning. She could barely summon the energy to dress before her husband returned home from work. After dinner, she sat in front of the T.V. and sank further into depression. It took all the energy she had to come to my office, but she made it. In the course of her treatment, I asked her to make a list of "reinforcing events," things she had formerly enjoyed doing, since it's very important for depressed people to schedule activities each day that they enjoy. I usually ask a client to incorporate at least one of these activities into his or her daily regimen. But this woman was too depressed even to attempt small pleasures such as taking a walk in the park, getting her hair styled, or meeting a friend for coffee. Stymied, I finally had her mentally rehearse the activities on her list. In a short time she was was able to translate the fantasies into reality, and her life became more enjoyable.

There are many uses for structured visualization. Another client of mine, a young law student, was scheduled to take the bar examination in a few months, and she was terrified of failing. After years of hard study to acquire her law degree, she felt her entire future hung in the balance and she would be devastated if she were to fail the exam and not get admitted to the bar. For several weeks I worked with her on visualizing herself being calm and relaxed while taking the exam, with her mind clear and alert, and the answers flashing to her readily. We also developed an image of the future, in which she went to the local newspaper office and saw her name posted on the bulletin board, listed among those who had successfully passed. Additionally, she saw herself receiving the official notice in the mail, and imaged her family congratulating her on her success. Happily, her image came true; she passed in the top quarter.

**Visualization and Sports**

Many coaches today are using the transformational technique of visualization as a significant part of the training regimen of their athletes. Charles Garfield, a former weightlifter, and a psychologist at the University of California in Berkeley, reported in *Brain/Mind Bulletin* (March, 1980), that he had used visualization with Olympic hopefuls to optimize their athletic performance. "The key," states Garfield, "is to visualize with the clarity necessary to really feel yourself in the situation...the central nervous system doesn't know the difference between deep, powerful visualization and the event itself, so the physical follow-up of the actual event is merely an after-the-fact duplication of an event already performed and completed in imagery."

Visualization works superbly for Chris Evert Lloyd, a top-seeded professional tennis player. Before every match she sits down, relaxes, and visualizes her every move, seeing herself return every one of her opponent's volleys and eventually winning the match. Her impressive record validates the effectiveness of this approach.

Mike Spino, Director of the Esalen Sports Center in Big Sur, California, coaches long-distance runners by using visualization. Runners image a big hand at their backs giving assistance during the race and providing something to lean into when fatigued. Spino believes that visualization techniques will be among the most important aspects of athletic training in the future.

The physiologist, Edmund Jacobson, famous for his relaxation technique, has demonstrated that, if a person imagines himself running, small but measurable amounts of contraction actually take place in the muscles used for running.

The Center for Accelerated Learning in Wisconsin conducted a study with students from four universities which proved that imagery improves learning and recall. According to this federally funded research, college students using mental imagery performed 12 percent better on immediate recall than students learning the same material without mental imagery. Furthermore, those using the imagery performed 26 percent better on long-term retention than those not using it. (Meier: Center for Accelerated Learning, 1103 Wisconsin St., Lake Geneva, Wis., 53147)

**The Mind/Body Connection**

Imagery works because *the subconscious cannot tell the difference between something that is strongly imagined and something that is really taking place in the physical world.* Anatomists have proven that there are pathways between the part of our brain where we store our pictures and the autonomic nervous system which controls involunary activities, such as breathing, heart rate, and blood pressure. There are also pathways from the autonomic nervous system to the glands, such as the pituitary and adrenal glands. What this means then, is that a picture in our minds has an impact on every cell in our bodies; thinking is not only an action of the mind, but an action of the entire body. In *The Body of Life* Thomas Hanna states:

> The nature of our thinking activity
> automatically determines
> the nature of our bodily activity...When we think the same
> thoughts of revenge over and over again, we are activating
> the muscles and glands of our bodies over and over again.
> When we repeat the same thoughts of disappointment over and over
> we are repeatedly stamping their motor power into the
> tissues of our body until they sag in forlorness.

Understanding this intimate connection between mind and body, we can rejuvenate ourselves physically and mentally through positive images. The greatest proof of this is demonstrated by hypnosis. In my seminars on self-hypnosis I have been privileged to witness the remarkable powers of the subconscious mind. On several occasions I have demonstrated the amazing control of the mind over the body by simple experiments such as painlessly inserting a hatpin a half-inch deep into the flesh of a subject's arm. When the hatpin is removed, there is no pain, no blood, and no afteraffect. The hole is completely gone within a few moments, and often the subject is not even aware that the needle was placed into his or her arm.

The subconscious is God-like; it is all-knowing and all-healing, and it will take care of you if you give it a chance. It never sleeps; if it did, you would not wake up in the morning because your subconscious takes care of your breathing, the circulation of your blood, your digestion, and every other bodily function while your conscious mind sleeps .

All you have to do is repeatedly tell your subconscious what you want, and it will then set about producing it. Unfortunately, many people, instead of working positively to achieve what they want, start worrying about not getting it. This sends out negative energy, and you end up holding a picture in your mind that you won't obtain the desired result. You can add more negative energy to that by telling your friends you wish you could have this or that but probably won't be able to. Then they, in turn, also hold the negative image. In this way you keep constantly giving a message to your subconscious mind *not* to bring you what you desire. The subconscious is a fertile field; whatever is planted is what you will reap.

**How to Visualize Creatively**

The art of visualization is a transformation technique which you

63

can use to obtain anything you want in life: love, prosperity, self-confidence, weight loss, a new job or car; whatever you wish. Imaging is a very precise methodology that can transform your life, but there are certain rules governing it. Here, then, are the steps to follow to create your own reality through creative visualization.

First, find a quiet place where you will be totally undisturbed and can completely relax. As studies in hypnosis demonstrate, the subconscious mind is very suggestible when we are in a relaxed state; thus, the more deeply you can relax, the more effective your visualization. If you are not accustomed to deep relaxation, refer to Appendix A or use the technique described in the chapter on self-hypnosis. Of course, never try to visualize when the radio or television is on or when the kids are running through the house. If you can find no other place where you can be undisturbed for at least 10 minutes, lock yourself in the bathroom.

### 1. Phrase it Positively

Before beginning your imagery make up a short, concise summary of exactly what you want, and always put it in the positive. For example, if you are working on weight loss, never say, "I will not be fat." This vibrates the cells in your brain connected with the image of obesity and reinforces the idea that you are overweight. Even though this may be true, don't strengthen the image by reminding yourself. Say, rather, "I am always going to be slim," or "I am becoming slimmer every day." If you feel inadequate, don't say, "I am overcoming my inferiority complex" and thus convince your subconscious that you have one, which will increase your anxiety. Instead, say: "I am becoming more confident every day."

A good friend of mine who is overweight invited me to her home for dinner one evening. When I arrived I found a picture of a huge hippopotamus pasted on her refrigerator door. "Betty," I said, "look what you're doing to yourself. You're telling your subconscious mind that you think you look like a fat hippo, and you're driving in the idea that you're overweight every time you walk by that picture." I suggested she clip a picture of a slender model from a Sears' catalog, paste a photo of her own face over the model's, and attach that to the refrigerator. "Let your subconscious know what you want," I told her, "not what you don't want.!"

Statements about your image should never be placed in the future, for example: "Soon I will be slender," or "I will get a job." Sure you will, but it may be another year if you phrase it so vaguely.

Some practitioners of visualization believe that you should express your affirmations as though you already have what you want.

I disagree, for that violates the next principle which is that images must be logical to reach the subconscious mind. It is not logical to say "I am now slender," if you currently weigh two hundred pounds. I suggest using the phrase,"I am becoming..." "Every day I am becoming more slender," or: "I am becoming more confident every day."

In dealing with specific things you desire, you can name a time limit: "By this spring I will have my new car." "I am now losing two pounds a week, and by Christmas I will weigh 120 pounds." "I will start my new job by the first of March."

Your positive statements can be written on 3x5 cards and placed by your bedside, on the bathroom mirror, or on the dashboard of your car; any place where you can see them frequently and repeat them, thus giving your subconscious mind ample reminders throughout the day. I like to put my imagery cards next to the alarm clock on my nightstand so that they are the last thing I see at night and the first thing I see in the morning. If you can visualize your desire at bedtime and fall asleep holding that thought, your subconscious will be able to work on it all night long, without any interference; and the process will be more effective.

### 2. Make it Logical.

The key to getting a message into the subconscious mind is: *If it's logical, it lodges; and if it lodges, you're hooked!* Remember, logical doesn't necessarily mean true. If, when you were six years old, you were told by Mom or Dad that you were awkward, clumsy, and not as bright as your sister, that suggestion would probably have been logical to you. After all, a parent is like a god to a child, so surely they knew what kind of person you are. Our personalities are formed by what we are told about ourselves in the process of growing up, even if it weren't true. If something is said to you that appears to be logical and you have no way to refute it, it becomes accepted by your subconscious and becomes a part of you.

On the other hand, if a statement is not logical to you, the conscious mind will simply refute it or throw it out, and it doesn't get past the psychic barrier into the subconscious. Thus, if your conscious mind cannot fully believe your image, it will not be accepted by your subconscious mind. For instance, if you wish to make some money, you should not say, "I'm going to earn a million dollars by the end of the year." For most of us this is completely illogical, so the subconscious will not accept it. If you want to lose weight, you shouldn't say, "I'll lose 30 pounds by the end of the month," because you probably won't be able to convince yourself you can.

### 3. Be Specific.

The more detail you can bring into your image, the easier it will be for your subconscious to carry it out for you. The subconscious mind is quite literal, and it needs to be given accurate directions. Of course, this is not always possible; but, whenever it is, take the time to think out each detail of your image. If you are looking for a new job, you may not be able to specify the particular building you would like to work in, but you can image yourself smiling and happy as you walk around your new office.

If you would like to move to a new house, think out in advance all the things that you would like to have in your home. Would you like a garden or a small yard that needs little care? Do you want a two-car garage, lots of storage space, a large kitchen, three bedrooms and two baths, a fireplace, a swimming pool? Be specific, but here again, make it logical. Don't ask for a house that is obviously beyond your means, thus making it illogical for you to obtain it.

Years ago when I planned to move to San Jose, California, to begin my post-graduate studies, I knew little about the city, having only driven through it a couple of times. I didn't have any friends there, so I had no one to advise me on a good location in which to live. But, instead of just driving around aimlessly in my car looking for an apartment, I sat down one morning and typed the following:

I am going to San Jose today to find an apartment that:
    is quiet so that I can study undisturbed.
    is close the university.
    is in a good neighborhood where I will feel safe.
    is spacious and clean.
    is bright and cheery and has lots of windows.
    allows pets.
    is in a price range of $—— to $—-.

I closed my eyes for a few minutes and imagined myself walking around in my new apartment feeling happy and content. Then I turned my image over to the Innate Power, knowing that It knew the area much better than I did and could lead me to the place I desired. By evening I had put down a deposit on an apartment which met my specifications exactly, except that the price was somewhat higher than I had wished for because my range hadn't been logical!

In the past when I had moved, I had searched for weeks for places to live by trying to do it solely on my own without asking for help from the great powerhouse of knowledge within us. I have learned that the method of directing and ordering my life by working with Spirit in a harmonious partnership is so much easier than doing things with my limited conscious mind. If you can learn to do everything in cooperation with this Great Force Within, your life can be so much simpler and harmonious.

At this point I must bring in a caution about dealing with cosmic laws. Using mind power and imagery means calling upon all the forces of the universe to attain what we want. These forces are extremely powerful and can create problems if used for wrong action, for this invariably brings suffering to the user. Those who use their mind power to bring harm or adversity to another will find that misfortune eventually comes to them. There is really only *one life* and anything we do to others, eventually comes back to us. We are all familiar with "black magic," which has been used for centuries to hurt others through mental powers. We might say that positive visualization is "white magic," and it works on the same principle. When using creative imagery therefore, heed this cosmic law: *Never manipulate the will of another!* If you do, it will boomerang on you and cause serious trouble in your life.

If you want a new house, for example, you can certainly image for one similar to an admired house of neighbors or friends, but never image specifically for *their* house. If you want money, never image that a specific person will give it to you, simply imagine it coming to you; receiving a check in the mail, putting a deposit in the bank, buying something that you want with the money. Leave it up to Spirit to select the means whereby the money will come; you don't need to concern yourself with that.

Ron, a salesperson, attended my seminar on imagery and immediately went home to imagine a potential customer signing a contract with him the next day. Ron relaxed in a living room chair and visualized himself driving to the customer's house, greeting the man as he opening the door, making his sales presentation, and seeing the man sign a contract for a very large deal.

This is a direct violation of cosmic law, for Ron was deliberately manipulating his customer's will. But, what is the difference between a salesperson's trying to persuade a customer to buy, and visualizing that purchase? The difference is that persuasion is done at a conscious level. We try to persuade people to do what we want every day of our lives, and there's nothing wrong with that, simply because people know what we are attempting to do and they can consciously resist it and defend against it if they want. On the other hand, when you image someone carrying out your desire, they are defenseless. They are your helpless victim and, without any conscious knowledge of why they are doing it, can easily fall under the power of your concentrated thought. In short, it isn't fair!

What Ron should have done in this case was visualize himself reaching a certain sales goal that month, or see himself telling his wife he had increased his commissions; winning the company award for topping the sales quota; depositing money in the bank; or even buying things he wanted with the extra cash. This would not have involved directly manipulating the will of another, but would leave it up to Spirit to provide the means whereby he achieved his desire.

A few years ago the newspapers reported the story of a man who saw a woman every morning on the elevator in his apartment building as he went to work. He found the woman attractive and, although he had never spoken to her, decided that he was going to marry her. Obviously, he was not interested in her qualities as a person, merely in her physical appearance. Since he had taken a course in mind control, he decided to image himself walking up the aisle with the woman and being married by his minister. The next morning he introduced himself to her and began a courtship, all the while imaging, without her knowledge, that he would marry her. Sure enough, within three months, his proposal and engagement ring were accepted and they were married.

I predict that this marriage will come to a disastrous end because this man deliberately manipulated the woman's unconscious mind and violated the cosmic law of *non-interference with the will of another*. Such misuse of the powers of the mind can create great havoc in an individual's life and in the lives of his or her unknowing victims. It is tantamount to a criminal act to take advantage of people without their consent!

This certainly doesn't mean that you can't image for a happy marriage. If you want to get married or be in a relationship, imaging for that is not only appropriate but desirable; just be careful not to image for a particular person. If you want to be in a relationship, the sensible action to take would be to make a list of the qualities you desire in a partner. This is something people seldom think of, and often they don't even know what qualities would be most compatible with their own personality. Sometimes people get married because they both like disco dancing or old movies, or some other inconsequential reason that doesn't mean much after the initial glow of romance has dimmed. The more similarities people have, especially in basic values such as honesty, thoughtfulness, and openness in communication, the more likely it is they will have a harmonious relationship. The more dissimilarity, the greater the potential problems because every difference can be a point of conflict.

Although it is a violation of cosmic law to image for a specific person, you can imagine yourself being in a relationship and doing things with a loving partner. You can feel your happiness at being with a person who really loves you, and you can imagine coming home after work and being greeted affectionately by such a person. If you wish to be married, it's perfectly ok to imagine yourself in a wedding setting and feel the happiness you expect to experience at that event, provided you don't imagine a particular person as your mate.

But, what if you've already met someone to whom you feel tremendously attracted? Let's say it's a man at the office. Though you must not specifically image him asking you out on a date or walking up the aisle with you, you are certainly free to send him all the positive, loving thoughts you want. There is nothing wrong with thinking loving thoughts because you are not manipulating someone by doing that, as long as you don't image him actually doing something with you. But you can be sure that he will pick this up, at least on the subconscious level, and will begin to respond warmly to you. You can visualize him surrounded by a lovely, soft, warm cloud of pink (the color of love) and see that color flowing from you to him. You'll be amazed at the results!

Some years ago I taught Concept-Therapy classes in the Bay Area with another instructor, Dr. Charles Craig. Mr. and Mrs. K. came to every one of our classes and usually sat in the front row. One day one of the students mentioned to me that Mrs. K. had told her she enjoyed the lessons but didn't care for the way I presented them. Mrs. K. couldn't seem to identify specifically what it was about my presentation that bothered her, but I strongly suspected it was Mr. K.'s intense interest in the classes, and his habit of discussing the material with me at every coffee break.

Realizing the importance of maintaining a harmonious relationship with all the students, and knowing my teaching would be disrupted if anyone were sending me negative vibrations, I thought it wise to rectify the situation. I liked Mrs. K. and had no adverse feelings toward her, so it was easy for me to mentally send her positive, loving thoughts. I found a class photograph with her picture in it, and I began talking to the photo, telling Mrs. K. that I liked and respected her and that she had no reason to feel threatened by me. I would say positive things like this out loud every time I walked by the picture, which I had put on my bedroom bureau.

At our next class, two weeks later, Mrs. K. brought a beautiful flower arrangement for the podium, which she handed to me, and she sat beaming throughout the class. Later she told Dr. Craig that she had been feeling very positive about my presentation and realized I was really a good instructor. Transformation had occurred merely from thinking positively, without any direct attempt to manipulate her will or thinking!

## 4.Time.

How long will it take to manifest your image? This is a variable that depends on your ability to concentrate and visualize, and also on the intensity of the problem. Naturally, if you are trying to change deep-seated feelings of inferiority, it will take a while; five minutes of visualization won't erase thirty years of negative thinking.

It has been established that it takes at least thirty-three seconds, as a bare minimum, for a suggestion to reach the subconscious mind. That's why television commercials are usually at least thirty seconds in length. Also, psychologists have determined that, on the average, it takes about twenty-one days to change a habit. The same principle applies to images. But, as your ability to visualize becomes perfected through repetition, you will find that many of your images will manifest sooner. Some people have reached a point, through continued practice, where some of their images come true within a few days, or even hours.

Feeling and emotion profoundly affect the amount of time it takes to get an idea into the subconscious mind. When something is said to you that has a severe emotional impact, it slams into the subconscious the instant you hear it. If, for example, a parent or teacher or boss says, "you're really stupid," that thought immediately penetrates into your subconscious mind. Unfortunately, when you begin working on changing a powerful suggestion like that, the same emotion is not behind it that was there when you originally heard it, so it takes longer to change, and requires repetition of the opposite concept.

How often should you image? A good goal to set is two or three times a day for 10 to 15 minutes per session. The more you practice and develop your power of visualization, the faster your images will come true.

## 5. Get the Feeling.

An important aspect of an image is the emotion behind it. The more feeling you can get into your visualization, the more convinced your subconscious will be that this is actually happening to you. *Act as if* you actually have the thing you desire and let your body experience the feelings you would have if you did. For example, if you wish to lose weight, *get the feeling* of how happy you will be wearing clothes that were formerly too tight for you, hearing people

70

congratulate you on your weight loss, looking at yourself in the mirror and feeling very proud of yourself. If you want a new car, imagine how good you will feel driving it down the freeway or pulling up in front of a friend's house in it. Remember, the subconscious can't tell the difference between something that is vividly imagined and something that is happening in reality, so very soon it will make it a reality for you provided, of course, that it is logical. The more capable you are of living in the feeling of the dream fulfilled, the greater is your capacity to receive your desire in actuality.

## 6. Take Some Action on the Physical Plane.

You must impress your subconscious that you mean business. If, for example, you are working on weight loss, cut down on your food intake. If you're eating like a horse, you can image all day, and nothing will happen, for your subconscious is getting a double message. If you wish to get a new job, begin looking at the classified ads, sending out resumes, and networking with well-placed friends. If you want to be in a relationship, go out to places where there is the opportunity to meet the type of person you want.

I stopped off one evening recently to visit with Doris, a young student of mine, and found her living room full of boxes containing most of her belongings. Doris is working her way through college and could only afford to live in a run-down apartment building filled with other students whose stereos blared day and night. She told me she could no longer put up with the noise and she was planning to move to a quieter building. I asked how that was possible on her limited income.

"Well," she replied, "I learned in your class that, if you want something to happen in your life, you first make an image, so I've been visualizing a new apartment every day. I decided packing up everything I don't immediately need would be taking action to convince my subconscious mind that I'm serious so that it will help me find a better place to live. Even if I have to stay here a few more months, I'm *acting as if* I'm moving, and that makes me feel better!"

Indeed, her subconscious got her message and did carry out her image shortly thereafter. Within a few weeks of my visit, Doris found a much nicer apartment a few blocks from the college at exactly the same rent she had been paying.

In order for an image to manifest, you must concentrate on it, and that is a protection. It means that any little fleeting thought we have will not automatically manifest in our lives—fortunately! If they did, we'd all be sorry for many of the things we created for ourselves and others through careless thinking. When something doesn't happen on schedule, our tendency is to indulge in negative thinking. For instance, if our partner doesn't arrive home at the usual time, our first reaction is to begin worrying that he or she has been hurt in an accident. Most of the time, we tend to think the worst, not the best. This sends out negative energy to the individual and, although it doesn't actually create the situation, it certainly doesn't help things. The best action under such circumstances it to sit down and take a few moments to visualize the person completely surrounded by a beautiful white light which protects them from any adverse forces. This is an ancient metaphysical method of psychic protection that has been used for centuries to insulate a person from negative thoughts and forces. Then, visualize your loved one smiling, perfectly safe, coming in the front door.

In order for an image to manifest, strong concentration is necessary and, the greater your ability to concentrate, the sooner your images will manifest for you. Concentration is an ability that can be developed; it is a learned skill just like any other. Training your mind day after day to focus on a particular image is a good way to develop your ability to concentrate.

Here then, in summary, are the steps for creating your own reality through imagery:

1. Phrase it positively.
2. Make it logical.
3. Be specific.
4. Take enough time.
5. Visualize the *end result.*
6. Get the *feeling* that you already have your desire.
7. Take some action on the physical plane.
8. Never manipulate the will of another.

Imagination is the key to all creativity and to all changes in your life and personality! It's not faith that makes all things possible, it's imagination. If you can imagine it, you can have it, provided only that it's logical. By sustaining mental images of any kind, (good or bad,) you will eventually bring about their manifestation in the physical world. You *are* what you imagine yourself to be! Whether you think you can, or you think you can't, you're always right. As Richard Bach wrote in *Illusions*, "argue for your limitations, and you get to keep them."

# seven

# HOW TO ACHIEVE PROSPERITY CONSCIOUSNESS

*Dreams are the seedlings of realities.*
*Your circumstances may be uncongenial*
*but they shall not long remain so*
*if you but perceive an ideal*
*and strive to reach it.*
*—James Allen*
*As a Man Thinketh*

Most people believe that wealth is either the result of an inheritance, or hard work and careful saving. This is a delusion. Statistics indicate that the majority of people in the United States, after a lifetime of work they often didn't even enjoy, end up barely able to survive on social security and a small pension, if they have one at all. Working a 10-hour day and saving diligently will not make you rich, but changing your ideas about money will. The starting point of all fortunes is a strong, positive idea, held constantly in the mind, which will eventually attract an abundance of money into your life. Wealth is an *attitude*, not the result of hard labor; thus, changing your attitude is the key to becoming rich.

Money is a man-made concept. It has no intrinsic fixed reality, but assumes the value people place on it at a given time. Your inner feeling about money determines whether or not you will have it, for that to which you are attentive is what manifests in your life. If you focus attention on the lack of money and the fear of poverty, that is what will get reinforced and become a reality for you. All human wealth is created by the human mind, and those who believe they deserve to be wealthy can create it.

A common myth about money is that there isn't enough of it for everybody. This is ridiculous because there are billions of dollars in the United States' economy, and you deserve your share. And, don't fall into the trap of resenting the affluent minority, those people who perhaps have amassed far more than their share. If you resent people who are wealthy, you'll end up resenting yourself when you make money. Focus on the positive; you will be contributing to raising the consciousness of others by serving as an example, and you can say: "Look at me, I've become prosperous by changing my thinking, and you can do it too." Remember, the money you make will be distributed to others and will help to prosper everyone you buy from or give money to.

But, you may say, "this is no time to make money. With the inflation index being what it is, it's almost impossible to acquire wealth because it already costs too much to live. " This is another myth, and it has been disproved in every economic crisis this country has ever had by people who refused to believe it. Many people today are making fortunes during this inflationary period, and you can be one of them. In bad times, in fact, there are so many discouraged people that a person with a success consciousness doesn't have to try so hard to make it. The particular state of the economy doesn't have to affect your personal situation if you learn to think positively and control your fears.

### You Deserve to be Wealthy

Before you can become rich, you must believe that you deserve it. It's impossible to convince your subconscious mind to bring you money if you have been programmed to the idea that you don't deserve it. We have all heard stories of people who had the ability to make a fortune but lacked the ability to keep it. Such people don't feel worthy of success; they don't think they deserve all that money, so they invariably sabotage themselves when they acquire it.

A man I knew in Toronto made a fortune as the owner of a camera store. When he had built his business to the point where he could retire and let his staff manage it, he suddenly began making mistakes: acquiring inventory he couldn't sell, firing his best manager, closing the store at peak hours. In a short time his business went downhill, and he went into debt. This so discouraged him that he began mismanaging his funds, and very soon he had to declare bankruptcy. He blamed his wife for the cause of his problems, divorced her, and started an entirely new business. Within a few years he was equally as successful and once again wealthy. Again, he couldn't handle it; he made some under-the-counter deals on the fringe of the law, acquired a bad reputation which damaged his sales, and eventually had to close his doors.

Sometimes it is not a fear of success but a fear of failure. A person may be going along well, accumulating money, and then begins to worry: "I'm making money now, but how long will it last? What if I lost it all? What if people stop buying from me?" and so on. We must constantly counteract these negative ideas with positive affirmations such as "I deserve to be wealthy" "I deserve happiness." "I deserve success." As soon as you get these thoughts firmly implanted in your consciousness, you have taken a giant step toward achieving wealth.

**Poverty Consciousness**

Before discussing the use of affirmations to develop a prosperity consciousness, let's look at some of the negative statements you may have acquired about money, for these need to be eliminated before you can make any progress. What did your parents tell you about money? What were their attitudes? Did they tell you that you were capable of earning a million dollars if you wanted to, or did they say: "You'll never amount to a hill of beans!" Write down on a piece of paper all the negative things you can ever remember your parents, relatives, teachers, co-workers, and friends telling you about money. It's important to take the time to do this because it will help you know what concepts have been programmed into your subconscious about money and, once you know them, you can set about systematically to remove them. You also may have programmed your own subconscious into many other negative ideas about money, for example: I don't deserve to make money because:

> I don't have enough education.
> I'm locked into a job which doesn't pay very much
> and I don't know how to do anything else.
> I married too young, and I now have too many
> responsibilities.
> I've gotten myself so deeply in debt that I'll
> never be able to get out.
> I can't be spiritual and make money too.
> I can't get a high-paying job because I'm female.
> I shouldn't make more money than my husband.
> My parents said I wasn't very bright,
> so I don't deserve it.
> My parents never had much,
> so I don't expect to either.
> I'm too young (or too old).
> I've never been able to get what I want,
> and I won't now.

If you are harboring ideas like these, you will eventually become discouraged and decide that you are not the person to make a lot of money. Although millions of people are seeking wealth and would like to have a financially secure future, they defeat themselves by this type of thinking. They have tried everything but changing their thoughts—the one thing that would make all the difference.

The power of thought is the only thing over which anyone has unquestionable control. A definite, strong idea, when it is held constantly in the mind, can actually change the biochemistry of the brain so that it will no longer be programmed to failure or defeat.

Thoughts are things; they have an electromagnetic reality, and they create their visible counterpart in the outer world. If you change your inner thoughts, your outer conditions must also change. *That's a law!* So begin now to have constant vigilance over your thoughts. Never again allow yourself to say "I can't afford it," rather say "I'm going to buy it; I'm planning for it now." Reverend Ike, the famous preacher who has inspired thousands with his sermons on prosperity consciousness, tells this story of his days in Harlem: whenever his friends saw a white man driving a big, expensive car through the area they would grumble about the honkies who kept them in poverty. Instead of complaining, Reverend Ike would say: "That's my car; there goes my car. I'm going to own one just like that." And now he does—in fact, several!

If you want to visit Europe, don't defeat your plans by thinking you'll never be able to afford it; instead say: I'm working on my trip to Europe now." And then set about collecting pictures and articles of places you would like to visit. Get a special box to hold your collection of information. Label it **My Trip to Europe.** Your physical experience will follow your thoughts, and your thoughts will begin to draw abundance to you. Each time you place an item in your box, the idea will become a little more possible, a little closer to its physical manifestation.

Some years ago, shortly after graduating from college, I worked as a therapist for a government-funded mental health agency that was very limited in its ability to pay its counselors. I was earning five dollars an hour and barely surviving. One Monday morning, Mike, a colleague, announced that he had spent the weekend in a workshop with Leonard Orr, a wealthy San Franciscan who was teaching people how to develop "prosperity consciousness." Mike said that Leonard had taught him how to make affirmations to attract money into his life, and he shared the method with me. Since I already knew about the power of the mind and had used visualization to change many other aspects of my life, I decided to try this specific method to increase my salary. Three weeks later, after having spent two years at the agency without a raise, my salary was increased by a few dollars. Excitedly, I told the director that my affirmations had worked.

"You call that prosperity?" he said cynically. "Around here it is," I retorted, but I knew that was only a beginning. I kept doing my affirmations, and small things began to happen almost immediately. An unexpected check refunding an overpayment on a loan arrived in the mail. Then I received a large tax refund which I had not counted on. Within a month, I was offered another job at a tremendous increase in salary.

Success is a much stronger concept than failure. It takes more energy to fail than to succeed because it takes a lot of concentrated energy to hold on to negative ideas about ourselves. And it drains us emotionally when we do.

Remember, in developing a prosperity consciousness, you will not only be up against your own resistances, but those of other people as well. Perhaps your parents or your mate will come up with some good reason why you can't possibly succeed at this, especially if they are insecure about your changing in some substantial way or doing better than they are. They may say things like, "this positive thinking stuff is too simple; it couldn't possibly work, and you're crazy to believe it." Ignore these comments and just keep on making your affirmations. Better still, don't tell people who are likely to resist your efforts. Work in silence and accomplish your goals without having to utilize your energy convincing unbelievers. It isn't easy to stay positive when everyone around you is complaining about poverty. Don't listen! A mental trick I use when people try to give me negative ideas (or even when I catch myself saying them to myself) is to shout *Cancel, Cancel!* in my mind, and then immediately supplant the negative thought with a positive one.

### Goals

Deciding on your goal is the first step in your program. Once you make a decision to be rich, you have taken a giant step toward achieving it. But, before you can attain wealth, you must know exactly what you want and what you intend to do with it when you get it. People don't really want money—after all, it's just a piece of paper—they want what money can buy. Once you have a strong idea of what you intend to do with your money, you can begin to focus on the specific amount you will need each year to accomplish your desire. When you make your affirmations, don't just ask for enough to survive, ask for sufficient money to enjoy your life, such as doing some travelling, buying a house, or getting some good stereo equipment. A friend of mine began making affirmations and told me that one of them was: "I will always have sufficient money to meet my needs." This is a limited concept and can result in barely surviving. A better affirmation would be: "I will always have more than enough money to meet my needs and to enjoy my life."

Since the first requisite is to discover what you desire in life, where you are going, and what you intend to do when you get there, ask yourself: "How much money would I like to have each year to create my life the way I would like it?" Don't just *read* this question; stop and take a moment to think about it. Make sure that you know what it is that you desire from life. Remember, ideas form the foundation of all fortunes. Once you make up your mind as to what you desire in life, you will have started a force into motion that will go out into the universe like a rocket, bringing back to you what you have asked for. The moment you choose your definite goal, and start making affirmations, you will observe a strange circumstance; the ways and means of attaining it will begin immediately to reveal themselves to you. Any dominating desire, goal, or purpose held firmly in the conscious mind through imagery and repetition of thought is taken over by the subconscious mind and acted upon, and it is thus carried out to its logical conclusion by whatever means are available. And Spirit Within will find the means. Ask yourself this question: "How much am I worth an hour?" If you think it's only a few dollars, then that's all you'll ever get. You must begin by raising your own self-worth and self-value. Put a price on your time and skills that demonstrates their true worth, and don't downgrade yourself by underestimating the value of your time and energy.

As the starting point of all achievement is the adoption of a definite purpose and a definite plan for its attainment, use the financial goals statement on the next page to write down three goals: those you wish to accomplish this year; those you will accomplish within five years; and your long-term, lifetime goals. Specifically state your goals even though these may not be totally clear at this point but, by programming your subconscious to specific objectives, the means will reveal themselves. If the method of achieving them is not presently clear to you, write down dreams and fantasies about how you could make money; for example, writing a book, winning a contest, being offered a new job at a larger salary, opening your own business, etc. The purpose of this exercise is to start the wheels of your subconscious into motion by making a commitment. After you've jotted down your methods (or daydreams), make a plan to manifest it. State the maximum time allowed for each step of the plan and describe precisely what you intend to do to reach your objective. Make your plan flexible enough to permit changes at any time you are inspired to do so. Remember that the Creative Power may present you with a plan far superior to any you can presently envision. Be ready, therefore, to recognize and adopt any superior idea that may later be presented to your mind.

Photocopy the Commitment page and place it where you can see it regularly, then repeat it aloud at least once a day. If you have people who believe in you and in your ability to create whatever you want in life, tell them about your plan. Then they too, can hold the image that your lifetime financial goals are coming true for you now.

## COMMITMENT

I, _____ ,
on this day of _____, 19____, hereby formally adopt the following financial goals:

By the end of this year I will be earning at least $ _____.

Five years from this date my yearly income will be at least

$ _____.

By _____, 19____, my net worth will be at least

$ _____.

I intend to retire from my job by _____, 19____, and devote my time to activities I enjoy, including:

_____

_____

_____

In order to accomplish the above goals, I pledge that I will spend some time each day visualizing and will make the following affirmations:

_____

_____

_____

/s/_____     Dated _____

79

## Treasure Map

Another way to impress the subconscious with your goals is to make a Treasure Map. After you have carefully thought out all the things you would like to do with the increase in money you are going to have, get a large sheet of posterboard. Begin looking through magazines and newspapers for pictures of your dreams. For example, an ad for the type of car you want, or pictures of foreign lands, a cruise ship or airplane flying to a dreamed-of vacation paradise, a beautiful new home, a harmonious relationship (symbolized by a family having fun together, or sitting before a fireplace), a successful executive going to the office, or whatever appeals to you. Make a collage of your ideals and put it on a wall where you can look at it frequently. This further impresses your subconscious with the idea that this is coming true for you now, and you will give it life and power by doing this. And, be sure to put yourself in the picture. Get a photo of yourself, and of others whom you will want to have with you when you achieve prosperity, and paste it on the collage. You will then have taken a powerful step towards realizing your goal.

## Using Affirmations to Attract Money Into Your Life

An affirmation is a strong, positive statement about something you want to manifest in your life. To affirm means to make something firm; thus, by stating your goal in a definite way, you are making it more firm to your subconscious mind. Affirmations are positive signals you are sending to your brain every time you say them so that, through the law of attraction and vibration, your subconscious can begin working to provide you with whatever you want. Writing down affirmations is an extremely powerful technique for reaching deeply into the subconscious, and is the fastest way to incorporate these ideas into your consciousness. It is far more effective than simply stating your goals. Some of the most dramatic changes in my life have occurred through using affirmations. Sometimes, in fact, the telephone has rung in the middle of my writing an affirmation, and it was the manifestation of what I had just written. The more you practice this technique, the more effective it will become for you.

The technique of using affirmations has been around for years; it's been taught in self-development courses and used by all positive thinkers and successful people. An excellent book on using affirmations to achieve prosperity consciousness is *Money Love* by Jerry Gillies, (Warner Books, 1978) and I strongly recommend that you purchase this book. Some of the affirmations in this chapter are from

Jerry's book. Another wonderful book, which is now a classic, is Napoleon Hill's *Think and Grow Rich.*

Many people, however, have not been successful in using affirmations because they already have so many negative ideas about themselves programmed into their subconscious minds that the positive affirmations cannot overcome them. Furthermore, they often don't know they are harboring these false ideas, so they faithfully repeat affirmations that don't manifest because their negative past programming needs to be eliminated first. I learned this important point from Leonard Orr's Money Seminars. Leonard discovered that all the negative material about money that you've absorbed through the years must be dealt with before you can become rich. The poverty consciousness that has been with you all your life will dominate unless you remove doubt so that prosperity consciousness can get a firm foothold. Write down your positive affirmations and, while you are doing that, listen carefully to your body and your inner feelings for any negative thoughts that negate your affirmation. Write these down too, then immediately refute them by writing down an opposite response. Keep on in this way until you can write the positive affirmation without getting any flack from your mind telling you it can't be true. In this manner you can clear your mind completely of negative ideas that say you don't deserve to be rich.

Here is an example of the kind of dialogue you might have with yourself:

*I, Vanessa, deserve to be wealthy and prosperous; and this is coming true for me now.*

"Oh, yeah, why should I be wealthy? I don't have any special talents, and I don't have a college degree."

*You know very well that you don't have to have a degree to become rich; Henry Ford didn't finish high school, and neither did Tom Edison, or a lot of other prosperous people. And as for special talents, you really have plenty of them; you've just never had a chance to develop them. What about your writing ability and the paintings you did in high school that your teacher said were so good, and the pottery you've designed? Besides, you may think up something unique to sell that nobody's ever thought about before.*

"Well, maybe you're right!"

*I, Vanessa, deserve to be wealthy and prosperous; and this is coming true for me now.*

"Maybe I could sell something special or buy a small business.

81

But Mom always said it wasn't important for women to make money because men don't want you to earn more than they do."

*Really? What a limited concept! Are you going to depend on someone else all your life? What's wrong with having plenty of money of your own?*

"Nothing."

*I, Vanessa, deserve to be wealthy and prosperous; and this is coming true for me now.*

"Why should I deserve it when there are lots of people out there barely surviving?"

*You deserve it because you're willing to take the time and energy to write these affirmations and gain control over your mind. You know that your subconscious will respond to whatever you program it with, so why not try it? Besides, your being poor isn't going to help all the other poor people.*

"Ok, I think you're right. I deserve it as much as anyone else, and I'm willing to work for it."

*I, Vanessa, deserve to be wealthy and prosperous; and this is coming true for me now.*

"I think I'm beginning to believe this. I *do* deserve money."

If, when using this technique, you get the same objection every time, invent an affirmation that is the opposite of that response. For instance, if you keep repeating, "I don't think I have any special talents," then write, "I deserve to be paid just for being the person I am," or, "my special talents are now being revealed to me."

It's advisable to write your affirmations in three persons and always include your own name. For example:

I, Vanessa, deserve to be wealthy and prosperous; and this is coming true for me now.

You, Vanessa, deserve to be wealthy and prosperous; and this is coming true for you now.

She, Vanessa, deserves to be wealthy and prosperous; and this is coming true for her now.

The repetition of positive messages to your subconscious and the refuting of negative ones is the only foolproof way of reprogramming your brain. Poverty consciousness is always the result of ideas others have given you, while prosperity consciousness is the result of the ideas you give yourself. As you use this procedure, negative ideas that you have buried in your subconscious will surface and be dealt with so that you clear your mind for wealth. It can save you years of trying to discover through psychotherapy, why you can't succeed. An actual chemical change takes place in the brain through repeated positive thinking. Once you start actively reprogramming your subconscious, thereby becoming totally committed and emotionally involved in creating your own prosperity, you are sure to succeed.

It's best to write a page of affirmations everyday, and don't just do it by rote, but really think about and visualize in your mind's eye the meaning of the words you write. Notice your resistances, feelings of doubt, or negative thoughts; and be sure to write them down. Then challenge them and counteract them with positive statements. In this way you will be able to discover why you have not been successful and how you have kept yourself from getting what you want. Once you feel that you've really overcome your negative programming, discontinue writing the negative and continue writing the positive.

As a step in convincing your subconscious mind that you deserve to have money, Jerry Gillies suggests in his book *Money Love* that you get a piece of paper, title it: "Five Reasons Why I Deserve to be Rich," and jot them down. We all have more talents and abilities than we usually acknowledge, and you probably have far more than your parents ever gave you credit for. Writing this down makes it more real to your subconscious mind.

Next, write down ten ways you can earn money. If you can always think of ten ways why you will succeed, you'll never be discouraged by temporary setbacks or by external conditions, such as high unemployment or the rate of inflation, and you'll never be broke. If you feel locked into a particular job and think you couldn't possibly do anything else, use this affirmation: *New opportunities for making money are opening to me daily.* Money can come from unexpected sources, and this affirmation takes away the restrictions on your earning potential. New vistas for making money surround you and, by affirming this on a regular, daily basis opportunities you have never even dreamed of will be placed in your path. The cooperation of others will become available to you, and job offers may suddenly appear as if by a stroke of magic. Your fears and doubts will disappear, and self-reliance and creativity will take their place. Somewhere along the way the idea or the job for which you have been searching will reveal itself to you. That has been the experience of most people who use affirmations on a regular basis.

Patricia R. used affirmations very successfully. She came to me for counseling because she was very dissatisfied with her job as a secretary in a local electronics firm where she had worked for six years. She was now at the top of her salary scale but, as a single parent of three children, Patricia simply couldn't afford any luxuries, and was worried about meeting her obligations. She was tired of scrimping and saving and wanted to explore other options so that she could earn more money  We discussed her returning to college and getting a degree, but Patricia felt this was not practical with three small children. I taught her the technique of making affirmations, and she agreed to practice this faithfully, and to especially concentrate on writing: *New opportunities for making money are opening to me daily.*

During December Patricia brought me a dried flower arrangement as a Christmas gift. I admired the artistry, and Patricia shyly admitted that she made the arrangement herself. She had developed this hobby in order to have something to do in the evening when she was home with her kids watching T.V. I pointed out that she was extremely talented and encouraged her to think about opening a small business selling the arrangements. Not being in a financial position to quit her job, Patricia decided to clean out her garage and convert it into a flower shop. She had some business cards printed, got a license, and began selling on a part-time basis. As her clientele grew and her self-esteem increased, she decided to take the plunge and applied for a small business loan to rent a store in a shopping plaza. Within a year she was making more money than she had ever earned as a secretary. An opportunity to make money, which she would never have dreamed of before, had presented itself to her as a result of her having diligently made affirmations, thus opening her subconscious mind to new possibilities.

**Affirmations for Women**

Women, especially, have been given some very negative programming about money. Often a woman is taught to believe from an early age that she shouldn't attempt to make a lot of money because she'll always have a man to take care of her. How sad to groom our female children to be parasites and depend totally on another person! Women have also been told that they will never make as much money as a man and they shouldn't bother trying. As a result, they often feel they don't deserve a high-salaried position and don't even strive for it. But highly motivated women can rise above the statistical world that pays women some sixty cents for every dollar a man earns, and can bring into their lives whatever they wish through the power of their thought. Some excellent affirmations for women can be found in Shakti Gawain's beautiful book *Creative Visualization*, and Sondra Ray's book: *I Deserve Love.*

Here are some affirmations especially for women.

I am a capable and successful person, and abundance is my birthright.

I am a powerful, dynamic, and wealthy person, and I am manifesting my abundance now.

I am self-confident, and my actions are decisive. I attract money to me through my desire to succeed.

I deserve to be as successful as the most successful man, and this is coming true for me now.

I am equal to the best of men, and there is no limit to my potential.

I am entitled to a large share of the world's wealth, and this is coming to me now.

The genius in me is released; I am now fulfilling my destiny.

My wealth contributes to my freedom, and freedom is my birthright.

I have enough time, energy, wisdom and money to accomplish all my desires.

I expect the unexpected; my highest good now comes to pass.

I am now becoming in touch with the Divine Plan for my life.

There are an infinite number of possible affirmations; adopt the ones that seem most fitting to you. Be sure to personalize them to fit your particular situation.

### Upgrading Necessity to Pleasure

Here is an affirmation used by Leonard Orr that I particularly like: *I work smarter, not harder.*

Freedom is something we all want and is probably one of the major goals of most working people. But, working just to accumulate enough money to retire on is poverty consciousness, and you'll probably end up living on a pittance. It's like saying "I don't deserve to have any freedom until I've put in so many years of hard labor." — Just like a prison sentence. There is no reason why we should have to follow a Biblical injunction written over two thousand years ago, admonishing the people of that time to "earn your bread by the sweat of your brow." But, many people are hooked to that concept. If that idea has been impregnated into your subconscious mind, the affirmation "I work smarter, not harder," can change it.

One of the best things you can do for your own prosperity consciousness is to lift someone else's, so another important affirmation is: *The more I prosper others, the more I prosper myself.* Money paid to others just means more money in circulation that can come back to you. A variation of this affirmation is: *A great deal of money is now coming into my life; I deserve it and will use it for my good and that of others.*

Because of our Puritan heritage, many people are programmed to the idea that money is only for necessities and it's frivolous or "unspiritual" to spend it for personal pleasure. If you feel this way, your life will be joyless and dull, and it's a good way to keep yourself in poverty. A life without fun, entertainment, or vacations is not worth living, and dulls the mind and soul. If you think spending money on yourself is evil, you may have to work on programming yourself to the idea that you deserve some pleasure.

A friend of mine dated a man who was the classical stingy bachelor. Although Fred earned good money, he was extremely cautious about every penny he spent and never bought any luxuries. He owned two suits, always ate at home, and refused to purchase birthday or Christmas gifts for his friends and family. The money Fred saved with his miserly habits went into a passbook savings account at 5-1/2 percent interest. With inflation at anywhere from 10 to 15 percent, Fred's money was slowly eaten up each year, guaranteeing he would end up as one of the many retirees who barely subsist. He is a prime example of a person with poverty consciousness. Fred is probably still manifesting it to this day because he's too stingy to buy a book like this or attend a seminar on prosperity consciousness. And, his life is a joyless one.

The most effective way to live is to balance your necessary expenses with some pleasurable spending. Realize that some of your money is yours to keep, to spend on things you really enjoy. Remember, you're not working just to pay your bills, but to enjoy your life. Because of their poverty consciousness, many people expand their expenses to meet their earnings so that there's never anything left over for pleasure. If your subconscious mind is getting the message that you only need money for necessities, it will arrange your affairs so that everything you earn goes for the basic things of life. So, take a step towards prosperity consciousness by taking some portion of your money every week, even if it's only five or ten dollars, and use it for yourself. Economizing all the time creates poverty consciousness. Learn to love yourself enough to realize you deserve the best in life.

To overcome the idea that you don't deserve pleasure, use one of these affirmations:

*A large part of all I earn is mine to keep for myself.*
*My income now vastly exceeds my expenses.*

### Personalizing Money

It's a good idea to personalize money instead of treating it as just a dirty piece of paper. That way you can develop an affinity for money that will attract it to you. For instance, you might think of money as a beautiful woman or handsome man who loves to visit you and can't get enough of you. In doing this, you could write:

*Money knows where I live, and she visits me daily.*
*Money is a lover of mine, and I treat her kindly so that she comes to see me often.*

If you are impersonal about money, it will be impersonal about you, and reject you. Everything in the universe has a life at some level, and money is no exception. Thus, make it into a reality in your life by giving it the respect you would give a dear friend or loved one.

**Increasing Your Prosperity Consciousness**

Prosperity consciousness is a spiritual idea, based on the principle that the Creative Power has provided infinite wealth, and a part of it is for our own personal use. There is a power greater than the power of conscious thought, but usually it's not perceptible to our finite minds. Recognition of this truth is essential for the successful development of prosperity consciousness. No great enduring success has ever been achieved by those who do not recognize and use the spiritual powers of the universe. The person with a connection to Spirit will find him or herself surrounded with an abundance of opportunities to amass wealth, and it will never be at the expense of others.

Another good affirmation for increasing prosperity consciousness is: *My income increases every day whether I'm working, sleeping or playing.* This is true because, if you have a savings account, even with only fifty dollars in it, your income is increasing every day because it's earning interest. It also means that you are programming your subconscious mind to give you valuable ideas each day so that your income will keep increasing. If you are working, most of your days involve a positive cash flow.

Make up a set of cards with your favorite affirmations printed on them and put them in an area where you can see them every day. You can put them on your refrigerator door, on the mirror in your bathroom, on the dashboard in your car, and on your bedroom nightstand. Even if you don't always read them, they'll be going into your subconscious mind every time you pass them and activate the brain cells connected with these positive thoughts. They will encourage you and remind you of your own capacity for attracting money into your life.

A part of developing a prosperity consciousness is feeling good about yourself in general. Here are some affirmations which you can use as needed:

**Self-Confidence**

*I am completely relaxed, self-confident, and self-assured in everything I do. I can accomplish any goal I desire through planning and self-motivation.*

**Concentration**

*I have the ability to focus my undivided attention on any*

87

*particular task at any time. I am able to concentrate deeply on anything I set my mind to. I can shut out all distractions and focus my entire attention on the problem at hand.*

### Problem Solving

*Every problem is an opportunity for me to be creative, and I am ingeniously creative. I consider every problem that confronts me as a new door to be opened. I begin every job thinking of new and better ways to accomplish the task.*

### Relaxation

*I am able to totally relax at will any time I wish. Regardless of the circumstances, I am a totally relaxed and calm person, completely in control of myself.*

### Energy

*I have all the energy I need for the day ahead. I am filled with rejuvenating life energy, and my total being is refreshed and energetic.*

### Composure

*I am in complete control of myself at all times. I am poised, relaxed and peaceful. I accept challenges and disagreement with calmness.*

### Affirmations for Salespeople

*I daily make valuable contributions to others by giving them an opportunity to own (name of product).*

*I am a friendly, pleasing person, and my customers like me.*

*I am highly disciplined and able to accomplish all of my daily plans.*

*People who enjoy my product are now being attracted to me.*

*Whenever people are unable to buy my product, I never take it personally.*

*The more I sell, the easier it becomes to sell even more.*

*I enjoy my job and get great pleasure from dealing with my customers.*

*The great universal forces are now helping me to achieve my goals.*

Affirmations are tools that can change your entire life but, if you don't use them, they don't work. You will not succeed if you constantly say, "Oh, I'm just too busy right now to sit down and do this." You must be willing to put the time and energy into this technique in order to experience the tremendous life changes that will begin taking effect once you do. You cannot begin this experiment and then immediately start checking yourself and say, "Wait a minute, I've written these for three days now, and so far I haven't received any money. This doesn't work." The subconscious never acts on a fleeting thought; it must be given constant programming until the ideas become firmly lodged in your mind and replace the negative ones already there. No enduring success will be achieved by those who are unwilling to put the necessary time and energy behind this. We must learn to think abundance constantly and hold steadily to constructive thought. It takes constant vigilance to gain supremacy over our unruly minds. But, the man or woman who will do this persistently and diligently is ensured of tremendous success in every area of life!

# eight

# ATTRACTING LOVE
# INTO YOUR LIFE

*To honor the self is...*
*to be in love with our own life,*
*in love with our possibilities for*
*growth and for experiencing joy,*
*in love with the process of discovery*
*and with exploring*
*our distinctively human possibilities.*
*—Nathaniel Brandon*
*To Honor the Self*

I once knew a very beautiful woman, who was intelligent, charming, well-educated, and a good conversationalist; yet she always became involved with men who treated her very badly. Marcia was going through her third divorce when she came to see me. Her first husband had been much older than she and totally dominated her. In this relationship she played out the classic Freudian "Electra complex" by subconsciously trying to get her daddy to love her. But it didn't work. Her father-substitute was so insecure because of her youth and beauty that he disapproved of her having any friends, occasionally followed her when she went on an errand, and refused to allow her to work in case she should meet a more desirable man at the office. After five years of this domination, and increasing headaches and backaches, Marcia finally divorced him for the sake of her psychological and physical health.

Shortly thereafter, she was pursued by a man her own age who, she discovered too late, was a cocaine addict. He had managed to conceal his habit so well that she was not aware of it until they had been married almost a year and she became increasingly suspicious about missing money and jewelery.

After a second divorce and four years of single life trying to recover from this emotional shock, Marcia married a high-powered executive who was incapable of being faithful to her and had constant affairs on the side. He was also a periodic drunk, and would verbally abuse her in a sadistic fashion about once a month when he went on one of his binges.

My counseling with Marcia uncovered the fact that she subconsciously hated herself and attracted men such as these because she thought it was what she deserved. Marcia came from a home where this beautiful, intelligent, sensitive woman had been treated as though she were an idiot and had been berated whenever she attempted to accomplish anything. Her parents' role seemed to be designed to demean and humiliate her, and she developed a tremendous inferiority complex. Little wonder then, that she attracted men who reinforced her "inner tape" and "proved" she was an unworthy and unloveable person.

We attract to ourselves whatever type of vibrations we send out. It is a cosmological law that people will treat you the way you treat yourself; if you hate yourself, you will not allow others to love you. When we have a low opinion of ourselves, we cannot accept the idea that someone can really love us; thus, we reject a person who does in favor of someone who will abuse us and reinforce our feelings of inadequacy. Our feelings about our self-worth go out into the universe like a magnet and pull into our environment the type of person who conforms to our own inner image. In *Actualizations* Stewart Emery writes: "If people's relationships with their own lives are unhappy, then their relationships with us are going to be unhappy as well. People who can't love themselves, can't love you either."

Perhaps, at the conclusion of a disastrous relationship, you have said to yourself: "I didn't know my partner was like that." Maybe you didn't on the conscious level, but the subconscious always knows; and it is that area of the mind which governs our lives. As Freud stated: "One subconscious mind understands another." At that level of awareness we know exactly what we are trying to accomplish, even if it is to destroy ourselves. If our old tapes are programmed for negative and destructive relationships, that's precisely what we'll get until we learn how to change those neurotic tapes.

Neurosis is perpetuated by the conflict between the idealized self (what one thinks one should be) and the real self, and represents the friction between desire and behavior, such as the following:

| DESIRE | BEHAVIOR |
|---|---|
| Assert oneself | Subassertiveness or Aggressiveness |
| Get work done | Procrastinate |
| Stop bad habits | Overindulge (overeating, drinking, etc.) |
| "Be this, be that" | "I can't do it" Resistance/Rebellion Self-destructive behavior (e.g., finding a mate who will abuse you.) |

Such behavior results in **guilt** which leads to:
Lowered self-esteem, which results in:
Verbal abuse of yourself, such as thinking: "I'm worthless,"
thus proving the negatively-programmed tapes.

And this self-hatred leads to:
Repression and denial.
Shutting down of feelings.
Inability to love others
Fear of being in touch with loving feelings
because of fear of rejection.
Loss of touch with the real self within
because of fear of seeing what you don't like
about yourself.

Neurosis is manifested by behaviors such as these:

**Conflict Radiating Inward:**
Psychosomatic illnesses (headaches, backaches, arthritis, ulcers, hypertension, coronary disease, etc.)
Depression
Anxiety
Sleep disorders
Chronic guilt feelings
Low self-esteem
Addictions (alcohol, drugs, food, etc.)

**Conflict Radiating Outward:**

Neurotic symptoms
Chronic procrastination
Phobias
Defensiveness
Subassertiveness/Overcompliance
Victim behavior
Chronic dissatisfaction
Fear of intimacy
Fear of loss of control
Nervousness, panic states
Narcissism
Social Withdrawal
Aggressiveness
Dance Away Lover Syndrome (constantly changing partners)
Sense of isolation and alienation

Obsessive compulsive behaviors, e.g.,: perfectionism,
I can't ever get it right; I can't ever relax.
Dependency (I have to depend on you because I can't
depend on myself, and I resent you for it.)
Helplessness (Tell me what to do, but I'll resist it
and prove you wrong.)
Indecisiveness (fear of making a mistake).
Power Struggle (hostile, hypercritical, punitive.)
Excessive materialism (I'm ok because of what I have.)

If you were a victim of parents who didn't know how to love you and are thus limited in your ability to love others, as well as yourself, this can be changed through the use of affirmations and mental imagery. If you were severely abused as a child, either verbally or physically, or find that you manifest a number of the neurotic behaviors on the list above, you would be wise to seek professional counseling to assist you in deprogramming your parental tapes. But, you can also help yourself, and thereby expand your ability to love. Let's begin with a method for raising self-esteem.

### Self-Love

Self-love is not the same as egotism. The egotistical or narcissistic individual really dislikes him/herself and has adopted an attitude of superiority as a defense against self-hatred. In our society, however, there is such a taboo against publicly expressing any type of love for oneself that people are actually afraid to care about themselves. Notice, for example, how difficult it is for some people to accept a compliment. They become embarassed and tongue-tied and try to avoid acknowledging it. If you truly care about yourself, you will always project this caring to others in your environment. The essence of love is caring enough about yourself so that you can respect and care for others.

People will treat you the way you treat yourself, so begin to examine carefully the way you have been acting towards yourself. For example, think of someone you regard as a very good friend. When you are with this person, you probably tend to be solicitous, interested, respectful, protective, and loving toward him or her. You have the other person's best interests at heart and you care about them. Now ask yourself: "Do I give myself the same tender consideration? Do I treat myself as kindly and respectfully as I treat my friend?" On the basis of your self-evaluation, you may have to answer truthfully, "No, I don't!" If this is your answer, ask yourself "why?" Aren't you as important as your friend? Then treat yourself that way! Observe the messages you are constantly giving yourself. Do you call yourself names, bark orders at yourself, chastise and berate yourself when you have said or done something you consider inappropriate? If so, you are only undermining yourself and decreasing your self-esteem.

Many people are in conflict with themselves because one part of them is at war with another part. A useful way to deal with this inner conflict is to recognize that we all have three parts: our inner child of the past, our adult self, and the internalized parent who, most often, is critical of our behavior. Although we may outwardly look and behave like an adult, those other two parts are constantly influencing and governing our behavior, and they must be recognized and dealt with.

Adults who, as children, have had critical parents, often have a very strongly developed, belittling inner parental voice which governs them, as the psychiatrist Karen Horney pointed out, by the "tryanny of should." They are constantly telling themselves, "I should do this," or, "I shouldn't have done that," "I should do better," "I shouldn't make mistakes," and so on. Recognizing, challenging, and questioning these dictates contributes greatly to freeing ourselves from the enslavement of our now internalized critical parent. And, at the same time, our inner child of the past, who is so often frightened and lonely, can be given reassurance by our adult part that we are really a worthy and loveable human being. Whenever you're feeling insecure, mentally talk to the little child inside you, and let her know that you, the adult, really care about her. Mentally love and nurture and console her.

As a child and teenager, I was in the habit of constantly berating myself for just about everything. After being with a group of friends or going to a party, I would come home and immediately start critically judging my behavior. If I had done something I considered to be dumb or socially incorrect, I called myself names for days and continually reminded myself of my inadequacy. Finally, I realized my self-condemnation was so severe I was making myself into a hopeless neurotic. I began to think of my critical, internalized parent as a person looking over my left shoulder, following me around and constantly belittling me. I vowed to get control of it and to put an end to this terrible guilt and self-condemnation.

I made a bargain with myself that I would allow myself to correct something I had done, once and only once. Once is a learning experience; anything after that is nagging and berating. So I simply labeled certain behaviors as inappropriate, rather than dumb, stupid, childish, or disgraceful, and told myself that I had now learned not to say or do that and had no need to repeat it. That is a corrective process, not a mental beating. After that, whenever the inner parent began to criticize me, I turned around and screamed, "Shut up!" at the top of my voice. Unless, of course, I was in public; if so, I screamed it in my mind. This may sound like a silly thing to do, but within three weeks I had gained total control over my self-condemnation and never again allowed my tyrannical inner parent to degrade or humiliate me.

Let the first principle in your program to increase self-esteem be this:

**Always talk kindly to yourself!**

Treat yourself as you would a loving friend and never, never call yourself names or denigrate yourself for inappropriate actions. As a therapist, I often assign homework to clients to give themselves a compliment every day. For many people, this is extremely difficult; they simply can't think of anything about themselves that they like.

How can we expect others to like us when we don't like ourselves? You can learn to become a loving friend to yourself, and even though you may not like some of your behavior patterns, you can always love your own inner self that is striving so hard to become a happy, self-actualizing person. In fact, with some people who are very lonely and have no one to love them, I tell them to repeat a statement every morning the moment they wake up, even before they open their eyes:

"I love you ——-(their name); you're a wonderful person." If you feel unloved, you will be amazed at how this simple affirmation will change your feelings about yourself. It's as though your higher self—that something deep within you—recognizes, respects, and loves you; and it's a marvelous way to begin each day! When you have a need for love, you can begin by supplying it within yourself.

**Give yourself at least one compliment every single day.**

A man once told me that he had cured himself of a painful back condition by simply placing his hand on his lower back several times a day and repeating, "I love you back. You're a part of me, and I will take care of you the best I can." The pain began gradually disappearing. How different this is from the approach most people take to such afflictions! Usually we hate the part of us that is giving us trouble, and would be rid of it if we could, thus concentrating negative energy on that area.

**Acknowledge and praise yourself verbally.**

No one can live without some feeling that they are a loveable and worthy person. Use some of the following affirmations to help you feel better about yourself.

I, ———, like myself, I am a loveable person.

I now feel loved and appreciated by my parents, my friends, and everyone who is important to me. (Even if you don't, repeated used of this affirmation will soon cause it to be true!)

My days are filled with love, joy and abundance.

I now give and receive love freely.

I deserve to be loved, and I am a loveable person.

Here are a few affirmations written by Shakti Gawain, from her wonderful book *Creative Visualization,* that are especially effective for developing self-esteem.

Every day I am growing more beautiful and more radiantly healthy!

The more I love and appreciate myself, the more beautiful I am becoming.

I am now irresistibly attractive to men (or women).

Divine light and Divine love are flowing through me and radiating from me to everyone around me.

I have all the love I need within my own heart.

I am a loveable and loving person; I am whole in myself.

I am kind and loving, and I have a great deal to share with others.

I am growing more and more attractive every day.

I love and accept myself completely as I am.

In addition to writing these or similar affirmations, make it a point to do something nice for yourself ever day. It need not be something that costs a lot of money, such as buying a new outfit, but some simple pleasure that makes you feel good about yourself and nurtures your spirit. This may be soaking in a bubble bath, taking a walk, window shopping, reading a novel, taking the time to watch the sun set, or just listening to some beautiful music that you enjoy. Nurture yourself in the same way that you would like someone else to take care of you. When you feel loved inside, you make room in your heart for love to come to you.

**Overcoming Procrastination**

Chronic procrastination is one of the most common self-defeating behaviors exhibited by people who have difficulty loving themselves. Many people cannot do what needs to be done because they use punitive measures and try to beat themselves into action mentally, and thus hook their rebellious inner child who refuses to cooperate. People who were overcoerced as children often learn procrastination as a defense and as a way of gaining some power in a powerless situation. Mother yells: "Get in here this very minute! Wash your hands right now! I want that room cleaned up immediately!" The child may not be able to refuse to do it, but s/he can take as much time as possible to fulfill the task: "OK, mom, I'll do it as soon as this program is over. I'm coming Mom. Just one more minute, and I'll come in."

In this subtle way the child is rebelling against such domination. Then, in later life, when the same person attempts to get her bills paid on time, clean out the closet, complete her income tax forms, etc., she yells at herself internally in the very same tone of voice used by the domineering parent. So what happens? She rebels and procrastinates until the very last minute, and sometimes beyond that, and her life gets into a mess. This is, of course, self-defeating behavior, which perpetuates self-hatred. She hates herself for being this way, but she is powerless to stop, because this neurotic behavior is driven by her inner child of the past, with whom she has never adequately dealt.

Taking care of the things in our lives which we tend to put off builds self-esteem. A part of self-esteem is the judgement we make about ourselves because of what we accomplish. If you are constantly

97

procrastinating, you are giving yourself plenty of opportunity to consider yourself incompetent or a failure. Routinely taking care of things is a way of clearing your mind and having more energy because you are not tying up a portion of that energy by holding something in the back of your mind that has to be done. By handling everyday tasks, you are handling your life; and it will convince your mind that you are an adequate person. Taking care of these tasks is a way of *being here now*, and living in the present. When you think of things that haven't been completed, you are in another space and not in the present, and can't fully enjoy your life. When you have a huge load of unfinished tasks, your mind can become so cluttered that you are unable to experience life totally because a large portion of your mind is bogged down with projects that are waiting to be done. Thus, in order to free your mental energy, begin doing the tasks that you have avoided for so long, and an increase in self-esteem will automatically follow as a result of your accomplishments.

Here is a systematic way to deal with chronic procrastination. Take a piece of paper and list on it the five most important things in your life that have to be done. Choose one of these to begin with, preferably the simplest. Then, estimate the length of time it will take you to do this project. A task can often be facilitated just by figuring out how long it's going to take. You may be surprised to discover that there are some items on your list which can be completed in fifteen minutes or a half hour that you have been putting off for weeks and needlessly tying up energy by worrying about it.

Next, ask yourself: "Why haven't I finished this task yet?" List as many reasons as you can think of. You probably have a mental picture that the task is very unpleasant, perhaps even painful, or so huge that it seems overwhelming. Or, perhaps you are uncertain that you have the skills to accomplish it. If so, write this all down.

In a new column list the solutions to each one of the obstacles you have stated. If you don't think you have enough information to complete the task, write down who you will have to contact or where you will have to go to acquire it. Then list the benefits you expect to receive as a result of completing this task. These may be internal, for example, increased self-esteem, a feeling of accomplishment, freedom from worry, more time for play. Or, you may also accrue some external benefit, such as praise from others, or additional income. Writing down these benefits will help increase your motivation.

Next, list the steps you need to take to complete the item. Break these down into very small steps. What is the first thing you need to do to approach this task? —Get out some papers, go into your desk, open

# WORKSHEET TO OVERCOME PROCRASTINATION

1. The Most Important Thing For Me To Do This Week Is:

   _____

2. I Will Begin Doing This: _____

3. Estimated Length of Time To Do This Is: _____

4. Reasons Why I Haven't Done It So Far:

   a) _____

   b) _____

   c) _____

   d) _____

5. Solutions To Each Of The Above Reasons For Procrastinating:

   a) _____

   b) _____

   c) _____

   d) _____

6. Steps I Need To Take To Complete This:                    Length Of Time
                                                             For Each Step:

   1. _____        _____

   2. _____        _____

   3. _____        _____

   4. _____        _____

7. Benefits I will Acquire From Doing It:

   _____

   _____

   _____

8. Visualize Yourself Doing It, and Then Finishing It. Notice How Good You Feel
   When It's Complete.

9. I Am Going to Give Myself the Following Reward When I Have Completed This Project:

   _____


SIGNED: _____        DATE:_____

99

the closet door, get some boxes for storage? List everything you need to do.

When all the steps are written down, determine how long each will take. Once you have done that, write a date of anticipated completion beside each step. If you have a large task that will take an entire weekend, such as cleaning out the garage, it's best to spread the work over several Saturdays. You probably can't motivate yourself to spend an entire weekend working in the garage, so make a realistic schedule, such as 1 to 5 p.m. every Saturday for the next three weeks. Remember, set yourself up to win!

Now, use your imagination; take a few minutes to relax and visualize yourself doing the task and completing it. This point is very important to increase your motivation. You may want to see yourself telling someone that you've completed it, and see them being pleased by this. Notice how good you feel when it's accomplished. This is one of the most significant parts of the program because, if you can accomplish the task in your mind, you will find it very easy to accomplish it in reality.

Finally, choose a reward you can give yourself when you have completed the project. It need not be something large, but it is very important to reinforce your efforts by rewarding yourself. Photocopy the worksheet on the next page to assist you in systematically overcoming procrastination; it will go a long way toward increasing your self-esteem!

**Attracting Love Into Your Life**

The necessary ingredient in attracting love is learning to live with, by and for yourself first. If you are single, you can create the conditions for love by being a loving person to yourself and others. Instead of being a time of loneliness and pain, being single can be a time of preparation. It's the best way to develop your own inner resources and really get to know who you are at the deepest levels of your being. Being alone can be a time of self-discovery and self-renewal if you see the possibility for such growth, and it's an opportunity to gain new certainty about yourself.

When a person merges with someone else they can lose sight of their true self and begin living through the other. Being single is a great challenge and helps develop the inner strength necessary to face life fully as a strong, independent individual. A person who has developed his or her own resources and skills is usually far more interesting than someone who has lived in the shadow of another and, when the right partner arrives, s/he will have something to give and something to share. S/he becomes a whole person who is unified

100

within his or her own center, and others will recognize and appreciate that.

Love, like other things in life, can be consciously produced. Just as you can make affirmations to increase your prosperity, so can you attract into your life the type of person you desire using the same procedure. Here again, the same rules apply; you must be careful not to violate cosmic law by manipulating the will of another. Therefore, make affirmations for the type of person you want, but *never specify a particular individual*. Leave that to Spirit and, if it is cosmically right for you to have a certain person, that will surely happen. On the other hand, if you try to force it through the power of your thought, there will always be some backlash.

The first thing to do before making love affirmations is to get a clear picture in your mind of exactly the type of person you desire. This seems self-evident but, believe it or not, many people have never consciously thought out what specific characteristics of another would be most harmonious with their personality. It's a good idea to get out a piece of paper and write these down. If you have difficulty, begin by thinking of your own qualities and make a list of those. Would you like your mate to have similar qualities, or would you prefer the opposite to counterbalance yours? For example, if you tend to be a spendthrift, you may want someone who is good at handling money, who can help curb your excessive habits. If you like classical music, you would probably prefer someone who also does; otherwise, his or her love of hard rock could drive you crazy! If you're athletic, it's best to specify someone who shares this interest, rather than a person who wants to stay home and read a book or watch T.V.

Additionally, be sure to list inner qualities you would like in your mate, such as honest, warm and loving, loyal, spiritually-inclined, kind, thoughtful, growth-oriented, mature, or any other attributes that appeal to you. Since this is such an important part of your affirmations, you may want to take some time to really meditate about the type of person you desire. Imagine how it would be if you had a relationship with such a person. Remember, the more specific you can be, the easier it is for your subconscious to fulfill your desire.

Another important question to ask before writing your affirmations is: "What is my intention?" Do you want to be married, or would you rather just live with someone for a period of time? Are you looking for a long-term, permanent involvement or just a temporary relationship? Perhaps you are so immersed in building your career right now that all you want is a fun-loving person to share some good times with you, who is also looking for the same level of involvement.

Are you the type of person who expects total fidelity and is willing to give the same to your partner? If so, list fidelity or loyalty as one of the qualities you want. Do you expect a monogamous marriage or would you prefer an open relationship with both parties able to see others? If you want marriage, do you want children? If you do, you should specify that you desire a mate who also wants this.

Be sure you have everything you want in your affirmations, but at the same time recognize your limitations. If you don't have the face and figure of a high fashion model, you're not likely to attract the equivalent of Hollywood's current Adonis. None of us are perfect persons, but there is a human tendency to think that we can attract super-stars, thus sometimes rejecting people who don't measure up to the fantasized image of what we want. Therefore, when you have completed your list, look it over and ask yourself if it is realistic. For instance, if you want a woman who is slender, blonde and beautiful, president of a large corporation, intelligent, educated, charming, and wealthy, then appraise yourself realistically to see if you would have enough to offer such a person.

Betty, a former client of mine, illustrated the importance of specifying everything you want in a mate. She divorced her husband of ten years because he was lazy, boring, and impotent. For seven of their ten years together, he had been almost totally uninterested in sex and would not seek help for his problem. So, when she began her affirmations, she focused on her primary interest of having a good sexual relationship. That's exactly what she got: a man who was extremely virile and well able to please her sexually. But he was also a Jekyl-and-Hyde type who was sweet and loving one minute and aggressively berating her the next. For two years she was on an emotional see-saw with him that did more damage to her self-esteem than ten years with her uninteresting husband. Finally, she could take it no longer. She decided the sexual satisfaction wasn't worth the mental abuse, and saved what little self-respect she had left by leaving him. At this point she almost lost her job because of her inner turmoil and had to enter psychotherapy to restore her confidence in herself. Before beginning affirmations for a more satisfactory partner, she worked for several weeks on a program to develop her self-esteem and convince herself that she was a worthy person and deserved better.

An interesting book which contains many affirmations for finding a partner is Sondra Ray's *I Deserve Love*, and some of the following affirmations were designed by her. Though these samples are all written in the first person, remember to put your own name into these, and write them in three persons: I, you and s/he. When you write your affirmations in the second and third persons, it gives you the feeling that "someone out there" also believes that you can have what you desire, and further impresses your subconscious mind.

I, Dorothy, deserve love, and the type of man I desire is coming to me now. He will be interesting, kind, warm and loving, faithful, financially stable, thoughtful, educated, emotionally mature; and he will like children.

I, Marc, deserve love, and the type of woman I desire is coming to me now. She will be intelligent, attractive, considerate, loving, athletic, interested in rock music, and able to move if I'm transferred.

I, Joanne, am now attracting a man who is tender, kind, responsible, intelligent, successful, open, and who has a sense of humor.

I, Paul, am now attracting a woman who is affectionate, passionate, interested in my kids, confident, joyful, and desires to stay at home and take care of the family.

I, Patricia, am filled with loving thoughts and magnetic power so that I can draw to myself the right type of relationships. There is an abundance of lovers who are just right for me, and I am attracting them to me now.

I, Larry, am now attracting into my life someone who is humorous and pleasurable, someone I can have fun with.

You can also specify approximately when you will meet the person you desire:

I, Jeannie, am now sending out the mental vibration of love, and the type of person I desire will be attracted to me. I will meet him this spring, and we will be married by the end of the year.

I, Bob, am now being led to the places where I will meet the type of person I desire. The universal law is now working so that I will be in the right place at the right time. My true love is now being attracted to me. We will buy a house together and be married by Christmas.

**Listening to Your Inner Voice**

Sometimes people have difficulty attracting love because they really are not ready to be involved with someone. This can be for a variety of reasons, such as being to busy to dedicate themselves to someone else. To discover any hidden thoughts that may be preventing you from finding love, you should divide your paper in half; use one side for the positive affirmations, and the other side for writing down any negative or counter-thoughts you may have. Listen carefully to your body while you are writing and notice if you get any negative reaction. If you do, write these down, and then write the counter-affirmations. For instance, Barbara began writing: *I now have the time and energy for a permanent, monogamous relationship; and this is coming true for me now.* Every time she wrote this, she could feel her stomach muscles tightening up. So, using the other half of the page, she wrote this dialogue with herself:

Oh yeah? You're far too busy developing your career to devote your time to someone else.

*That may be, but I'm very lonely, and I want a permanent, monogamous relationship and this is coming true for me now.*

Stop kidding yourself. You couldn't handle it. He'll be demanding of your time, and you'll resent it.

*Maybe you're right. I guess it's just the wrong time for me to try for a long-term goal. I'd better concentrate on my career first.*

This mental dialogue led Barbara to revise her affirmation to: "I, Barbara, deserve love; and I am now attracting into my life someone I can have fun with, who will not be too demanding of my time."

## Affirmations to Overcome Fear of Love

Sometimes people cannot attract a new love because they have been hurt in the past, and are afraid it may occur again. If this is preventing you from finding an appropriate partner, use some of the following affirmations.

I,——, am now free of the past regarding my negative emotional experiences. I have learned a great deal from them and will not repeat the same mistakes.

I, ———, no longer focus on the losses I have suffered in the past. Instead, I am confident that my next relationship will be a beautiful and harmonious one.

I, ———, deserve to have someone who will love me exclusively, and the type of person I desire is being attracted to me now.

I, ———, forgive ——— for the way s/he treated me, and I am now releasing this experience into the universe and will no longer suffer from it.

I, ———, do not need to get even with men (or women) any longer. I can let them love me.

I, ———, am willing to accept love and stop resisting. It is safe to surrender to love.

I, ———, now take full responsibility for my actions, so I no longer feel guilty for anything I have done in the past.

I, ———, am no longer angry at women (or men). I feel very loving towards them, and am now attracting a loving person into my life.

I, ———, am now releasing my past experience with ——— and am no longer affected by it.

I, ———, still have love in my heart for ———, but, since s/he is no longer interested in me, I am now completely accepting of this and wish him/her well in the new relationship.

## You Deserve Love

Many people are hampered in their ability to find a loving mate simply because they don't believe they deserve one. If you feel this way, use your affirmations to convince your subconscious mind that you are worthy of love.

Beverly, a lesbian, made an appointment with me because she felt so unworthy that she had been unable to find a lover for the past three years. For five years prior, she lived with a woman who suddenly decided she could no longer handle the enormous difficulties of being gay in a society that condemns those who love people of the same gender. Beverly's former lover lived in fear of being discovered, losing her job, and having family and friends turn against her. Finally, she told Beverly that she wanted to end the relationship, get married to a man, and try to live a "normal" life without deception. Beverly was devastated by this and felt suicidal. In her despair, she went home and revealed to her parents for the first time that she was a lesbian. Tragically, they were horrified by this revelation, told her she was an "abomination before the Lord," and said they never wanted to see her again.

Because of her deep feelings of unworthiness and her fear of being hurt again in a relationship, Beverly was unable to find another gay woman to love. During psychotherapy she fought hard to regain her dignity and self-respect as a person, even though her life-style was different from the majority. She came to realize that what was important was not how others viewed her, but how she viewed herself. She knew that she was not "less than human" because she loved women, and decided that she must be true to her own inner self and not the dictates of others. Once her inner conflicts were resolved and she could accept herself, she began making positive affirmations for love, and found a new relationship within a few months.

## Affirmations for Overcoming Negative Programming

If you have been the victim of negative concepts, such as "you're stupid," "why can't you be like your big sister," "you're really awkward and clumsy," "you're not very attractive," etc., you could use some affirmations like the following to change these suggestions. Remember, you must find as many reasons as possible as to why you deserve love so that your subconscious mind will be reprogrammed to the idea that you are really worthy.

I deserve love because I am a warm and loving person and have helped many people in my lifetime.

I deserve love because I have a great deal of love to give and am willing to share it.

I deserve love because I have a lot of assets and really care about people.

I deserve love because I have had a great deal of suffering in my life, and I don't intend to suffer any more.

I deserve love just because I am alive, and I'm entitled to happiness.

I think highly of myself and therefore it is easy for people to love me.

I now feel secure about my ability to attract the type of person I desire, and I deserve this.

I deserve love because I am a loving person.

Affirmations, properly done, can help create your life exactly as you truly desire it to be: happy, prosperous, totally healthy, fulfilling, joyous, creative and, particularly, filled with love. By reprogramming the barriers to love that you may have, both consciously and subconsciously, you can enjoy the complete fulfillment and satisfaction that always accompanies real love.

# nine

# HOW TO BE HEALTHY
# ALL YOUR LIFE

Yes, there really are methods of ensuring that you will be a physically healthy person your entire life, and need not end up a sick, crippled invalid in your older years! It is a myth, which is increasingly becoming disproven, that old age must mean incapacity, senility, and a host of degenerative diseases. We of this generation are very fortunate to be living in a time when science and holistic health practitioners are discovering methods of prevention and self-healing which can not only prolong one's life, but allow a person to enjoy the golden years free from the so-called "diseases of old age." You may not be aware of how much you can do to slow down, or even reverse, the changes that usually accompany aging; but it will take some work on your part to bring about this happy ending to your latter days on earth. No matter how young or old you may be, now is the time to start.

According to the present knowledge of the constituents of good health, here are the six ingredients for staying healthy all your life:

1. Stress reduction: proper thinking
   and expression of feelings.
2. Proper nutrition.
3. Regular exercise.
4. Adequate rest and relaxation.
5. No substance abuse (addictions).
6. Social contact: Love/Family/Friends.

**Emotions as a Cause of Disease**

> *Everything depends on one's opinion.*
> *We suffer according to our opinion.*
> *One is as miserable or as happy as one*
> *believes oneself to be.*
> *—Seneca*

The new medical model recognizes that the mind is a factor in every disease, except perhaps the very few ones caused by external agents, such as poisons. Dr. Kenneth Pelletier, author of *Mind as Healer, Mind as Slayer,* believes that all states of illness are in some way psychosomatic; not in the sense that they're imaginary, but in the sense that they all involve mental and physical factors.

Dr. Andrew Weil, author of *Health and Healing*, states that: "Agents of disease are not the causes of disease. The underlying causes of disease are *internal*." And: "All illness is psychosomatic. The mind and body are interdependent and together can cause or prevent sickness."

The intimate connection between the state of the mind and the state of the body, has finally gained acceptability. In scientific circles the study of this field even has a fancy new name: *Psychoneuroimmunology,* and a new professional journal by the same name, but it is based on a very old idea. It has been known for centuries that a person's psychological state can affect their health, but science is finally discovering how it really happens. And that is leading to new ways to treat disease, particularly the methods now being utilized by holistic health practitioners; those who treat the whole person, not just the body.

One of the major proponents of psychoneuroimmunology is Dr. Robert Adar of the University of Rochester Medical School, who has edited a book under that title. Some two dozen medical experts contributed chapters in which they examined the role psychological factors play in bringing on disease. One chapter examines the way certain kinds of psychological stress can set the stage for infectious diseases; another examines the relationship between depression and cancer, and still another explores the role of the emotions in arthritis. Stated at its simplest, the conclusion is: our health is controlled by our brain.

Aided by new biochemical techniques and a vastly expanded understanding of neurochemistry and immunology, new studies prove that our emotions affect our nervous system, glandular system (hormone levels, adrenaline production, etc)., and the response of our immune system; all of which affect a person's susceptibility to a host of illnesses. Studies have revealed that emotional reactions can suppress or stimulate disease-fighting white blood cells and trigger the release of adrenal gland hormones, and endorphins, morphine-like chemicals produced by the neurotransmitters of the brain, that in turn affect dozens of bodily processes. It is becoming increasingly accepted that emotions are *necessary components* of the cause, as well as the treatment, of most illnesses. The new studies show that virtually every physical problem—from the common cold to cancer and coronary disease—can be influenced, positively or negatively, by a person's mental state.

Today, there is a great deal of talk about the connection between stress and disease—but what about the components of stress? Basically, stress is comprised of negative emotions, such as worry, anxiety, depression, feelings of hostility, guilt, anger, and so forth. The researchers speculate that chronic indulgence in negative emotions creates a lowered resistance to disease by interfering with the ability of the immune system to fight it. Fear creates stress, and any anxiety will cause muscles to contract and blood vessels to constrict. Illness sets in when blood cannot be transported freely to the body's organs and nerve tissues to provide oxygen, nutrients and anti-bodies, and to carry away and dispose of toxic waste materials.

Diseases are not haphazard; they don't just come out of the blue and strike a person one fine day without any antecedents. Current research is demonstrating that, if you are prone to getting a disease, the type you contract will be something specifically related to your personality, which is called the theory of "psychosomatic specificity." The reason for this is that different emotions act on different parts of the body and produce differing chemical reactions, resulting in specific types of diseases. Every thought produces a physiological effect. The effects they produce are chemical substances such as adrenaline and ACTH. When your thoughts produce chemicals such as these at the wrong time, or in excessive amounts, the result is an impaired immune system.

**Coronary Personality**

Much has been written for example, about the type of person most prone to coronary disease, the Type A personality, who is hard-driving, impatient, hostile, demanding of himself and others, highly competitive, and usually involved in multiple projects. "Cynicism, better than any other word, captures the toxic element in the Type A personality," according to Redford Williams of the Duke University Medical Center. "If a more trusting attitude can be learned," he said, "help for heart patients may be on the way." Williams and his colleagues did a series of experiments to determine this. According to psychological tests, the "hostility" scores of Type A people were significantly higher than those of Type B. High scorers were 50 percent more likely to have coronary artery blockages than were low scorers. After analyzing the responses of 1,500 people to 50 items, Williams found a concise unifying theme: cynicism, a contemptuous distrust of human nature and motives. When we are frequently hostile, excessive secretion of norepinephrene, a brain chemical, contributes to our risk of hypertension, arteriosclerosis or heart attack.

## Cancer Personality

In his book *You Can Fight For Your Life: Emotional Factors in the Causation of Cancer,* Dr. Lawrence LeShan, a clinical psychologist, identifies four typical components in the life histories of the more than 500 cancer patients with whom he worked:

The patient's youth was marked by feelings of isolation, neglect and despair, with intense interpersonal relationships appearing difficult and dangerous.

In early adulthood, the patient was able to establish a strong, meaningful relationship with a person, or found great satisfaction in his or her vocation. A tremendous amount of energy was poured into this relationship or role. Indeed, it became the reason for living, the center of the patient's life.

The relationship or role was then removed—through death, a move, a child leaving home, a retirement, or the like. The result was despair, as though the "bruise" left over from childhood had been painfully struck again.

One of the fundamental characteristics of these patients was that the despair was "bottled up." These individuals were unable to let other people know when they felt hurt, angry, hostile. Others frequently viewed the cancer patients as unusually wonderful people, saying of them: "He's such a good, sweet man," or "She's a saint." LeShan concludes: "The benign quality, the "goodness" of these people was in fact a sign of their failure to believe in themselves sufficiently, and of their lack of hope."

Keep in mind that not all of these traits apply to every cancer patient.

Another element of LeShan's description, that cancer patients tend to be prone to feelings of hopelessness and helplessness even before the onset of their cancer, has been confirmed by other studies. Considerable evidence has shown that the immune system is impaired in people who feel unable to cope with adversity, and a feeling of helplessness may be a key factor in vulnerability to cancer. When we feel depressed and helpless for extended periods, the released chemicals suppress the ability of the immune surveillance system to screen out cells that lead to cancer.

Dr. Carl Simonton, Director of the Cancer Counseling and Research Center in Fort Worth, Texas, and his former wife, Stephanie Matthews-Atchley, have specialized in working with cancer patients

110

for a number of years, using traditional methods, plus guided imagery. Together with James Creighton., they have written an excellent book, *Getting Well Again*, which is a step-by-step guide to overcoming cancer for patients and their families. In this book Dr. Simonton reports that, almost always, the cancer is triggered by the loss of a serious love object, occurring one year to 18 months prior to the diagnosis, in people who have suffered a loss early in their lives. Usually there is a major loss, such as a job, a death, or divorce, followed by deep feelings of sadness, anxiety and hopelessness. When there has been an early childhood loss, this triggers the feelings of hopelessness that accompany the second loss.

There is now confirmed evidence that grief, loneliness, helplessness and negative attitudes like anger and fear can measurably depress immune system functioning. Antibody production, thymus function, and the activity of T and B helper cells, are all weakened by negative thoughts. When we feel our problems are beyond our control, the hormone cortisol, increases, and makes us more vulnerable to infections.

People with strong needs to dominate have depressed immune defenses when they face certain stressful situations. The person with hypertension, for example, may believe he must constantly be ready for battle, so his body behaves as though it were going to be attacked and keeps his blood pressure high. Hypertension is more likely to occur in persons who feel as though they must always be ready for combat with some outside source, although their aggression is usually held in check.

When we feel we're in danger, (such as anticipating a fight with our boss or mate), our heart rate speeds up, the fats, cholesterol and sugar in our blood stream increases; our stomach secretes more acid, and our immune system slows down. All of these sudden changes are an enormous strain on our system. Over time, this strain leads to symptoms such as gastrointestinal distress, high cholesterol levels, insomnia, headaches, and back pain. It also leaves us more vulnerable to infections.

In *Studies of Ulcerative Colitis*, Dr. G.L. Engle reported that bleeding episodes in ulcerative colitis came and went as patients experienced feelings of helplessness during some stressful situation, or perceived new strength when a crisis was overcome.

We can easily see the direct relationship of our emotions upon our bodily functions when we experience strong feelings such as fear and anger. Suppose, for example, you are in a situation that scares you, such as giving a speech before a large group of people. The brain is given the message: "I'm threatened in this situation." This message goes directly to the autonomic nervous system (ANS), the involuntary system that controls our heartbeat, breathing, digestion, and other internal activities. The ANS automatically responds to the brain's message of threat by producing more adrenalin, speeding up your heartbeat, activating the sweat glands, reducing the saliva, tightening the stomach muscles, and increasing the activities of all the other bodily processes which accompany fear, temporarily throwing your entire system out of order.

Or, let's say you become very angry at your boss. Your brain sends this stress message to the ANS, and the internal organs are immediately activated to war production. Blood is driven out of the abdominal cavity to the lungs, the muscles, and the brain, bringing them their needed increase of energy for action. Your blood pressure rises. Carbohydrates are moved out of storage in the liver and muscles and converted into fuel for action. The adrenal glands, which are the fighting glands, pour their stimulating hormones into your blood stream, and your entire body is made ready for flight or fight. Primitive man would have done one or the other, but modern man can usually do neither. Instead, he puts a smile on his face and tries not to reveal his true feelings. Naturally, this whole procedure puts the body under tremendous stress and interrupts the homeostasis of the body, making it more vulnerable to disease. If this indulgence in anger occurs repeatedly, the constant rise in blood pressure may lead to hypertension, or possibly a stroke. Or the chronic muscular tension can cause arthritis or toxicthyroidism. Or the disturbance in carbohydrate metabolism may eventually produce diabetes, or any of a number of other diseases may begin to manifest.

Suffice to say that when a person indulges in strong, negative emotions, such as fear, anger, chronic depression, jealousy, worry, or thoughts of revenge, every system in the body becomes disturbed. If this is repeated long enough, the organism will eventually break down. And that is the major cause of disease.

In his remarkable, well-researched book *Who Gets Sick: Thinking and Health* Dr. Blair Justice states: "The major premise of the medical model that we have all been programmed to for several centuries is that germs are the cause of disease. This is not true. There is no single cause for disease. Rather, disease is multi-factored and originates in many things a human being does in their daily lives. This means that disease is ultimately under the control of the person, and not some haphazard thing. It's what we choose to do as we travel down the highway of life that makes the difference. It is not some unfortunate contact with a single evil agent, such as a germ or virus that is lurking in the bushes and springs on us. The traditional medical theory of one-germ, one-disease continues to support the idea of evil germs, or of bad luck—it just happened, and you're the victim. The doctor, of course, is the savior, so "fix me."

Even Louis Pasteur, who gained prominence in the late 1800's for his discovery of germs, recognized that the host (the person) had to be in a certain state of debility before germs could settle into the body. He spoke of the disease process being dependent on the underlying health of the body to begin with.

**Tuberculosis**

Dr. Justice states: "For example, although the presence of the tubercle bacillus is a necessary condition for tuberculosis, other factors must be present for the disease to occur. The majority of adults today are tuberculin positive, meaning they are infected, although they never show clinical signs of the disease. For every 100 Caucasian Americans now becoming infected with the tubercle bacillus, 99 percent will not develop the classic pulmonary disease. In his pioneering study on stress, Dr. Hans Selye observed that reactions to psychological threats could trigger a person's latent tubercle bacilli."

**Herpes**

Many people carry the herpes simplex virus that erupts in cold sores. It is now known that psychological stress can precipitate outbreaks of this normally latent Type 1 herpes virus. Researchers from the University of Pennsylvania found that students who were frequently unhappy had a higher incidence of cold sore episodes during the year. The greatest effects were found among students with high loneliness scores, and those who were depressed. Students facing exams have also been reported to have an increased incidence of cold sores.

Psychiatrist Janie Kiecolt-Glaser of Ohio State reported that over-stressed medical students studying for important examinations showed poorer immune function than they did during summer vacations.

In another study by Dr. Kiecolt-Glaser reported in the Journal of Behavioral Medicine, 9(1),5-21, it was found that medical students had decreases in helper T-cells on the day of exams. But, when half the group were taught relaxation exercises, their T-cells increased. The percent of their disease-fighting T-cells could be predicted by how frequently the students practiced relaxation!

113

On a cellular level studies show that the ability of our lymphocytes and antibodies, our resistance to infection, is affected by how we appraise stressful events and react to them. Dr. Blair states: "Disease or dysfunction is the body's way of saying that we have failed to adapt, adjust, or change to meet the situation, and we have done so at the price of physical or mental disturbance... A good attitude and the ability to get along with other people, characterizes those with a low frequency of illness."

## AIDS

Although it is almost a universal assumption that all people who develop AIDS will eventually die, the fact is that a great many persons with AIDS have lived well beyond the usual 3 years, although we seldom hear about it. An interesting case, with well-documented medical data, of a man with AIDS who became entirely symptom-free after utilizing metaphysical principles, was reported in the March, 1985 issue of NEW REALITIES magazine. He is only one among a number of long-term survivors of AIDS. Only a small portion of infected persons become sick during any type of viral epidemic, and it may well be that the HIV virus only causes disease in people whose immune systems have already been compromised by their lifestyles, such as taking drugs, (including antibiotics), drinking too much, poor nutrition and, in general, putting their systems on overload. Psychologist Hal Knooden of New York City, observed that all of those patients who developed AIDS reported experiencing unresolved stressful situations prior to the onset of the disease.

According to researchers at the National Institute of Health Conference in San Francisco in 1986, new studies of people with AIDS, and certain types of cancers, are proving that there is a link between attitude, stress hormones, and the immune system's resistance to disease. For instance, studies have shown that men who *think* they have swollen lymph glands, but don't, show changes in the number of their infection fighting T-cells. Aggressive and resourceful AIDS patients appear to survive longer than patients who are helpless, hopeless, and socially passive, according to preliminary findings by Dr. Lydia Temoshok of the University of California, San Francisco.

## Smoking and cancer

We have been told repeatedly, and it is even printed now on cigarette packages, that "smoking causes cancer, heart disease and lung disease." This simply is not true. Smoking is a risk factor which is correlated with these diseases, but correlation does not mean cause.

114

If smoking actually *caused* cancer, then every single person who smoked would have to get cancer but, in fact, is is not even one-third, which would be 33 percent. Statistically, only 30 percent of all cancers are attributed to smoking. So what about the approximately 70 percent of smokers who don't get cancer? What protects them? We have been given the idea that science has isolated cigarette smoking as a single cause of cancer, all by itself; but it isn't. The majority of smokers do not develop lung cancer!

Nicotine may be viewed as a co-carcinogen, that is, a substance that is activated in the presence of *other* cancer-causing elements. But, by itself, it cannot cause healthy cells to become cancerous. Carcinogens in the environment and in our diets may produce cancerous changes in our cells, but the evidence suggests that malignancy will not occur unless other risk factors are present and our immune systems are depressed.

Dr. Simonton states: "We all have cancerous cells in our bodies at all times, and smokers have a slightly higher number than non-smokers. But our immune system recognizes these malignant cells and destroys them. The real question is: why does that stop happening in certain individuals and they go on to develop cancer?"

In *Who Gets Sick?* Dr. Blair states: "Although heart disease and all other leading causes of death and disability today require the presence of *multiple risk factors*, there is still mounting pressure to explain the appearance of most chronic diseases on the basis of such single variables as cigarette smoking, alcohol consumption, or exposure to other hazardous substances...These substances by themselves do not "cause" disease, although this assumption is widely held despite the fact that the majority of those thus exposed do not succumb prematurely to the disorder in question."

Whether the disease is cancer, coronary problems, or AIDS, it appears that "cofactors," not single causes, are responsible.

Cigarettes alone will not cause cancer or heart attacks, but cigarettes, plus other abuses may, because our risk is increased by introducing this toxic substance into the body. But a *key* co-factor in all illness, which is now the subject of intense research by the new science of biological and molecular psychology, is our thinking: how our emotions affect our health and can contribute to making us sick. Since we now know that the brain regulates all bodily functions, including the important immune system, our thinking processes are being increasingly implicated as one of the most important contributing factors in the creation of disease.

In *Health and Healing* Dr. Andrew Weil states: "This point must be stressed: external, material objects are never causes of disease, they are merely agents waiting to cause specific symptoms in susceptible hosts. Rather than warring on disease agents with the hope (in vain, I suspect) of eliminating them, we ought to be more concerned with strengthening our resistance to them. Illness, it seems, occurs more from our general vulnerability, than from external agents.''

Since disease is not so much the effect of toxic, external forces, or the germs in the air, or in our bodies, why do some people get sick and others don't when they are exposed to the same agents? What decides whether a person is at risk of acquiring a particular disease, and under what circumstances will a person so disposed develop a disease?

Our susceptibility to disease how now been convincingly linked to the way we cope with life; and that means how we view the events and situations that occur everyday. The way we react to the daily stresses of life is the *central determinant* of whether or not we will contract a disease. If we have poor coping skills, high stress, poor nutrition, no exercise, and chronically indulge in negative thinking, then the internal balance of our bodies is easily upset and we are less resistant to disease. The way we react to what Freud called ''The psychopathology of everyday life'' can determine whether we will get an infection, or remain symptom-free. Since most of the microbes that afflict human beings are already present in our bodies, they will erupt into disease *only* when other risk factors lower our immunity. Smoking is a risk factor, and so is constant worry, hostility, envy, anger, hard-driving competitiveness, anxiety and depression.

Of course we cannot control the world, but we can control our response to it. How does it affect a person's health if they wake up each morning dreading to go to the office? Or—dreading to come home at the end of the day? What does it do to the immune system to continue in a job or relationship we hate? J.I. Rodale, founder of *Prevention Magazine* wrote a book in 1970 with the interesting title: *Happy People Rarely Get Cancer.* On the other hand, the unhappy person is the target for any kind of illness.

Three personality factors that make one prone to disease were identified in a very informative book: *The Complete Guide to Your Emotions and Your Health* by Emrika Padus and the editors of *Prevention Magazine.*

**1. Control:** How much we believe we need to control is a key determinant of how distressed we will be if we appraise a situation as being beyond our control. Some people have high needs for power, that is, they must not only control the situation, but impress and influence others.

116

**2. Need for Approval:** Some people have strong affiliative needs; they want to be loved and accepted by everyone, and they are always seeking approval, and become depressed when they don't get it.

**3. Perfectionism:** A third group is made up of those who need to perform perfectly in whatever they do, and of course they're doomed to failure because nobody can be perfect.

We all have to face a great many crises, and sometimes even very severe traumas, in the course of living our life. But, it seems it is not so much the number or severity of the stresses in life that create illness, but how we react to them. Far more important is the interpretation we give to the situation and our resultant response. Dr. Hans Selye, author of *The Stress of Life,* an endocrinologist who is one of the world's foremost researchers on stress, came to the conclusion that it is not the stress per se, of a particular situation that impacts us, but how we appraise that situation. What causes disease is not the difficulties of our lives, but how we cope with those problems. For example, suppose you're driving on the freeway and someone passes you giving you a rude gesture. If you just drive on and let the incident go by thinking something like: "It's too bad some people are so uptight today that every little thing elicits a hostile response," you're not likely to experience any physiological consequences of any significance. However, if you chose to fight back by doing the same to him, or some other angry response, (besides risking getting attacked), your entire nervous system will become alarmed and tense and you will discharge adrenalines that increase your blood pressure in anticipation of combat. If you happen to be a coronary candidate, the result may be a heart attack. The question then is: What caused your death? The driver? His insult? No, you caused your own death by allowing yourself to become tense and angry by someone else's actions.

According to Dr. Albert Ellis, psychologist and author of *A Guide to Rational Living,* emotions have very little to do with actual events. In between the event and emotion is a realistic, or unrealistic, assessment of it through our inner dialogue, and it is our self-talk that produces the emotions. Our own thoughts, directed and controlled by us alone, are what cause anxiety, anger, guilt, tension, depression and hostility. In a word: stress. We assume that things are done to us, such as "She makes me angry...being lied to makes me see red...the boss makes me nervous...people talking like that depresses me," etc. But these things are not actually done to us: we choose our own reaction through our interpretation of the situation and our consequent self-talk. The way out of this is through self-awareness. Tune into

117

your body: if you become aware that reacting negatively to the daily hassles of life is creating tension, fatigue, headaches, backache, and so forth, you might want to reexamine your responses and learn to become more tolerant towards the inappropriate behavior of others. When people change how they are looking at problems, and see them as challenges, or simply temporary setbacks, and understand that they can at least control how they react to them, this helps to restore and maintain a proper biochemical balance in the body.

Our reactions are determined by our basic beliefs and perceptions. Learning to control our thinking means learning how to appraise difficult situations in such a way as to reduce their impact on our nervous system. In order to do this, we must be aware of our internal dialogue, and try to interact with events as positively as possible. Thinking about events negatively, or acting evasively in order not to have to deal with them, sets us up for illness. In a word: *Attitude is everything!*

According to studies reported in *Your Emotions and Your Health* the personality traits that help people confront stress the most are the 3 C's: Commitment, Control and Challenge; three traits which add up to what psychologists call "hardiness," and it's the hardy people who survive longest and are the most resistant to illness.

1. *Commitment* to work, family, self-improvement, and other important values.

2. A sense of personal *Control* over one's life.

3. The ability to see change and stressful events in one's life as a *Challenge* to master.

It is the people who are able to act decisively and positively towards the daily challenges of living who beat illness, whether it's cancer or coronary disease. Their positive thinking and enthusiasm induce T-cells and other lymphocytes to increase in number to devour malignant cells and other germs. In such people, the daily hassles like traffic congestion, breaking a favorite vase, or spilling the wine while having dinner with the boss, are simply minor problems in the ongoing drama of life; they refuse to be upset about it. They know, for instance that, while waiting for the traffic to move, they can either lean back and enjoy some good music, or an educational cassette tape, and get home feeling relaxed and having benefited from the time alone in which they can unwind or, they can become tense and angry at the situation, and arrive home *at exactly the same time* with elevated blood pressure and pulse rate, ready for a fight with whomever is waiting. You can play it either way — and you get to choose! As clinical researcher Stewart Wolf, M.D., has said: "Disease is a way of life, it is the end result of the way that people react to life's problems."

We should also mention here the power negative suggestions have to adversely affect our health. We are continually being bombarded through our advertising media with suggestions that we will get this or that illness, and we must become aware of the subtle influence these concepts have on our subconscious mind, and learn how to counteract them. We are assaulted on a daily basis through television, magazines, newspapers, etc., with suggestions that it's "cold season;" the flu is going around; do you have a headache? Arthritis? Sinusitis? Stomach ache? Constipation? and so forth, so that the cells of our brains our kept in a state of constant vibration concerning these illnesses. These continual negative suggestions become lodged in our subconscious mind and, if repeated frequently enough, increase our stress, lower our resistance, and can actually contribute to setting us up for disease. The answer is to become consciously aware of this type of brainwashing and set up a counter-response to such negative suggestions. Wouldn't it be wonderful if we turned on our T.V. set and heard the announcer say: "Nine out of ten doctors recommend relaxation training, meditation, taking a day off for mental health, or just giving love to someone as a remedy for headaches, backaches, arthritis, and other ailments." Unfortunately, no one would sponsor such an announcement; there's no money in it.

Harboring in our mind constant fears of major health catastrophies such as cancer or heart attacks, can help attract these diseases to us. Instead, use the principle of imagery and positive affirmations,and concentrate on ideas that are health and vitality oriented.

Finally, all disease comes down to one thing: we have impeded the flow of energy through our bodies. Why? Because we are afraid! Fear is the basis of it all. We are afraid to be vulnerable, we are afraid to be hurt, afraid we might appear stupid, afraid we'll be rejected by someone, and afraid to reveal who we really are. With all of this holding back; the constant defending, constant distrust, constant "shoulds," we stop the proper flow of our vital energy, and set ourselves up for disease. In health or disease: *Attitude is everything!*

**The Healing Power of Love**

Love is good for your health! Recent research has shown that lovers get fewer colds because the germ-fighting white blood cells perform better when a person is in love. Being in love also makes your lactic acid level drop so you have more energy. Everyone knows lovers can get by on very little sleep; your body feels more energetic, and

119

there's a bounce to your step when there's romance on your mind.

Of course, it is not possible to always be in love, and some people, for whatever reason, do not have a partner. But love is not limited to one's mate. There are many avenues and opportunities to give and receive love. If we don't have anyone in our life right now to give us love, then we must begin by giving love, and the law of cause and effect ensures that it will come back to us. Extending one's self into the community in some way, and giving love to others is a necessary ingredient for health; it is medicine for the soul and body. Almost any kind of loving relationship can contribute to good health, including love for our pets. For those who don't have a mate, family, or pets, getting involved in a group and helping achieve the goals of that group, establishes social bonds and prevents us from focusing solely on ourselves. Isolated people are more susceptible to illness.

An excellent definition of love is given by Dr. Scott Peck in *The Road Less Travelled:*

*Love is the will to extend one's self for the purpose of nurturing one's own or another's spiritual growth. When we grow as person's we need to work at it, and we work at it because we love ourselves and want to improve and elevate ourselves. And it is through our love for others that we want to assist them to elevate themselves. Love, the extension of the self, is the highest act of evolution. It is evolution in progress. The evolutionary force, present in all of life, manifests itself in mankind as human love. Among humanity love is the miraculous force that helps and heals and elevates all of life.*

Love and friendship are great reducers of stress. When we know we have people we can turn to in trying times we feel stronger, more confident, less isolated, and more in control of situations. Knowing we have supportive people in our lives, whether it's our mate, our family, or our friends, provides a feeling of security and hope, which helps reduce stress. Sociability of any kind is worth cultivating for the sake of our mental and physical health. Limited and restricted expression of affection and tenderness towards others almost guarantees a compromised immune system. Mounting evidence is showing that people who belong to a network of community, friends and relatives are happier, healthier, better able to cope with life, and remarkably resistant to emotional and physical ills.

**The Healing Power of Touch**

Research is now confirming what psychologists have been saying for years: Being touched in an affectionate way is vital to our well-being. Dr. James Hardison, psychologist and author of *Let's Touch*, says: "It is through touching that we are able to fulfill a large

120

share of our human needs and, in doing so, to attain happiness. By touching someone we can affirm our friendship or approval, communicate important messages, promote health and bring about love." But the problem is, we have been trained to put up a lot of barriers to being touched. "For one thing," says Dr. Hardison, "our society tends to equate touching with either sex or violence. Consequently, many people avoid the simple acts of touching—pats on the back, heartfelt handshakes, cordial hugs—that affirm good-will."

Our lives would be barren and impoverished without the kind of touching that implies real caring. Touch is a means of communication so crucial that its absence retards growth in infants, and it has direct and important effects on the growth of the body as well as the mind. Researchers have found that premature infants gain weight faster and leave the hospital sooner if their mothers touch, rock, and talk to them. A study done at Rush-Presbyterian-St. Luke's Medical Center in Chicago showed that babies touched at regular intervals by their mothers left the hospital an average of 4 days earlier than normal. The massaged infants also showed signs that their nervous systems were maturing more rapidly; they became more active than the other babies and were more responsive to such things as a face or a rattle. They also gained more weight, although they did not eat more than the others, and this seemed to be due to the effect of contact on their metabolism. The new research suggests that certain brain chemicals released by touch may account for these results. Other research shows that all babies benefit from touch. Studies by Dr. Theodore Wacks, a psychologist at Purdue University, showed that infants who experienced more skin-to-skin contact had an advantage in mental development in the first six months of life.

Reaching out to touch other human beings in a caring fashion should be a part of our everyday lives. For those who live alone, and may also work in environments where touching others is inappropriate, loving and nurturing a pet can provide the same fulfillment for some people. Pets offer us love no matter what. Lacking that, there are organizations available to everyone (or volunteer work) where we can share friendly, touching companionship...It's medicine for our soul!

*Let Your Food*
*Be Your Medicine*
*Let Your Medicine*
*Be Your Food.*
*—Hippocrates*

# VITAMINS: NECESSARY OR SUPERFLUOUS?

The second most important component in maintaining good health is proper nutrition. Unfortunately, in this technological, over-populated, over-polluted, over-"chemicalized" society, we can't get it from food alone. Much of the food we buy today goes through approximately 40 different processes before we actually eat it, and each one of these processes reduces its nutritional value. The regulatory agencies in the United States allow over 3,000 different chemicals to be added to our foods, and the average American eats *five pounds* of these toxic chemicals every year, and all of these synthetic products stress the immune system. The FDA, and some doctors, have pronounced that practically no one needs diet supplementation if they just eat a balanced diet. Few biochemists and other health professionals who have really studied nutrition, believe this potentially dangerous assertion. And the chances are the doctors who declare that are not very healthy themselves.

Dr. Carlton Fredericks, a renowned nutritionist, and author of many books on the subject says: "The person free of disease is abnormal in our society." The U.S. is the sickest nation on earth; believe it or not, we come in at 93rd place, according to a study reported in *Prevention Magazine.* Yet we have more doctors than any other nation.

If you want to "just get by" with your health, then don't take vitamins. If, however, you would like to be in optimum health, then it is absolutely necessary that you take supplements every day. Dr. Fox, author of the Fox diet says: "I give all my patients a Vitamin Analysis and dietary survey. I have yet to find a patient with the proper amount and balance of vitamins and nutrients."

## What Do Vitamins Do?

Vitamins enhance the body's natural ability to restore and maintain its health. We could not live without vitamins, because they are of enormous importance in keeping the body well. Vitamins are a nutritional necessity because they act to protect us from over-active chemicals in the atmosphere, in our foods, and in the things we put on our bodies, and from our body's own incomplete chemical reactions. These chemicals can actually do physical damage to our cells, like starting hardening of the arteries by injuring the walls of the blood vessels. Vitamin protection actually neutralizes these chemicals, and is called the anti-oxidant and free radical scavenger effect.

Vitamins detoxify, absorb and carry out of the body toxins and harmful chemicals that don't belong there. They also neutralize specific brain toxins that build up in all of us and interfere with our normal brain activity, thereby improving our brain function. Vitamins also supply parts for the enzyme systems that regulate the body's chemical reactions. This is called the nutritional need.

If it were possible to live in an environment where the soil were free of chemicals and had not been stripped of its nutrients, and the air we breathe were uncontaminated by poisons, then we would not need supplementary vitamins; but this is decidedly not the case. Synthetic hormones and growth regulators are regularly injected into foods, and deplete them of their natural vitamins. The nutritive value of many of our foods is destroyed before we even buy it. We may go to the supermarket and purchase a fresh fruit, such as an orange, or grapefruit, and feel that thereby we can get our daily quota of Vitamin C. This is not necessarily the case. The fruit has usually been injected with chemicals to give it a nicer color, and of course it has been sprayed with a number of insecticides, all of which affect its nutritive value. One investigation of oranges taken from a supermarket showed that half of them had *no Vitamin C whatsoever*, and many of them had only about 40 percent of what they should have. And fresh foods such as these are grown in soils increasingly depleted of minerals, force-grown with high-nitrogen fertilizers, and sprayed with poisonous chemicals. As a result, our foods are deficient in important minerals, such as zinc and selenium, and our bodies consume vitamins fighting off the effects of pesticides.

Americans are eating more processed foods, which is often the equivalent of eating a chemical factory, and many essential nutrients are destroyed or removed during processing. Our foods are now stored longer, so that the vitamins deteriorate during shipping and storage. Yet we are deluded into thinking that, if we just eat properly, we will get all the vitamins and minerals we need. In our technological society, this is no longer possible. As a result, a large part of the population suffers from mineral and vitamin malnutrition, which results from the modern American way of eating. And this is not just among the poor, who may be deprived of proper nutrition, but among middle-class Americans, with access to an enormous variety of food.

Although many doctors still state that "People don't need supplements as long as they eat a balanced diet," the nation's M.D.'s are notoriously ignorant about nutrition. In the Journal of the AMA (August 8, 1980), Richard a Wright, M.D. admitted: "Most medical schools devote less than three hours of total instruction to nutritional deficiency and therapy." There is far, far more time spent in the average medical school on the question of malpractice insurance, than on the subject of nutrition. In the light of current estimates that six out of the ten leading causes of death in this country are diet-related, that's shocking! A "Cholesterol Awareness Study," sponsored by the National Heart, Lung and Blood Institute, in 1986 surveyed both the public and physicians by telephone. Amazingly, the results showed that consumer's understanding of the relationship between diet and heart disease far surpassed the doctors. Only 64 percent of physicians agreed that reducing high blood cholesterol levels can help prevent heart attacks, while 75 percent of consumers thought it was effective in preventing heart disease. Even more surprising, only 40 percent of the doctors believed that cutting back on high-fat foods was important, while 50 percent of the public knew that eating high fat food increases the chances of having a heart attack. So don't be surprised if your doctor thinks taking vitamins is a joke, or a harmless but worthless indulgence. He or she simply hasn't had the training to think otherwise.

David Rubin, M.D., a professor of preventive medicine at Georgetown University, sees the medical profession's current disinterest in nutrition as the result of a system of education that's hospital-oriented, a system "where there are acute problems, and you teach students how to care for people who are already sick." *(Caveat Emptor,* July, 1980.) The focus is not on prevention, but on cure of already-established illnesses.

In addition to over-processed foods, many other environmental factors deplete our supply of vitamins. For instance, people who overindulge in coffee, cigarettes or alcohol burn up or flush out large amounts of vitamins and minerals. Along with excessive sugar, too much coffee seriously depletes the body's stores of thiamine (Vitamin B1). The result is jittery nerves, irritability and a feeling that you're out of control. White sugar, white bread, and other refined foods are deficient in the B vitamins and minerals. Sugar also robs our body of essential nutrients in the process of being metabolized, so eating any refined food creates a need for extra B vitamins, and it is also hard on our body's supply of calcium. Experiments have also shown that refined sugar, which is sucrose, depresses the immune system. And that in turn impairs the body's ability to fight infections. Some of the symptoms of this deficient nutrition are the symptoms people experience on a daily basis: headaches, insomnia, fatigue and irritability.

Drugs also increase the bodies needs for vitamins and minerals. Medications such as aspirin and other anti-inflammatories greatly increase the body's need for Vitamin C. All drugs put additional stress on the body, and thereby increase the need for the other anti-stress vitamins such as the B-complex. Antibiotics alter the normal intestinal bacteria. Problems that can occur as a result are decreased intestinal utilization of a variety of nutrients, including calcium, magnesium, folic acid and Vitamin B12. Studies have proven that women taking oral contraceptives run a high risk of Vitamin B6 (pyridoxine) deficiency. Recognized experts in the area of research advise that 25 to 30 mgs of B6 be taken daily by any woman on the pill.

Stress also steals our nutrients. Anxiety, anger, and every other kind of stress, overtaxes the adrenal glands and robs the body of Vitamin C. "Stress causes a skyrocketing of nutritional needs," says Arthur C. Hochberg, Ph.D., a nutrition-oriented psychologist in Bala Cynwyd, Pennsylvania. One of the B vitamins in particular, pantothenate, "is withdrawn from the body at an alarming rate and must be replenished," Dr. Hochberg asserts. Additionally, "during stress there is an increased withdrawal of minerals from the system."

Dieting, the great American pastime, also places stress on the body. Since many people are already eating foods that are deficient in proper nutrients, when they go on a diet and reduce their intake, the nutrients already lacking are virtually eliminated, making a person more susceptible to disease.

**The RDA's**

The RDA's, or Recommended Daily Allowances of essential vitamins and minerals, are the daily amounts that, in the opinion of the government's Food and Nutrition Board of the National Academy of Sciences, are "estimated to exceed the (nutritional) requirements of most individuals." The RDA's have been established to minimize the risk of severe disease-causing nutritional deficiencies, *and nothing more.* According to Alfred E. Harper, Ph.D., professor of nutritional sciences and biochemistry at the University of Wisconsin, "The RDA's are not designed to cover nutritional needs that may be elevated as the result of disease, stress, or the chronic use of certain drugs." Also, "RDA's *do not take into account losses of nutrients that occur during food storage and preparation. The RDA's are the minimum requirements. Minimum requirements produce minimum health. Unfortunately, this is what most Americans have. If this is all you want, then don't take supplements. However, if you would like to be in optimal health, then you would be wise to exceed the RDA's."*

The government says the RDA's are "adequate to meet the known nutritional needs of practically all healthy persons." Most people, however, are not healthy and, if you want your health to be only adequate, then don't take vitamins. Or, if you have some bad habits such as eating sugar, not exercising, smoking, breathing polluted air, eating processed foods, being under stress, and drinking alcohol or coffee, then you must realize that you are depleting your body's store of vitamins and minerals on a daily basis. If these are not replenished, you are impairing your immune system and jeopardizing your health.

## Are Vitamins Harmful?

*One of the arguments constantly given against vitamins is that they can be toxic. According to Drs. Carolyn Reuben and Joan Priestley, authors of Essential Supplements for Women* to be published in 1989 by Putnam & Sons, "There is a government agency which takes reports called in by doctors on side effects and toxicities of drugs and vitamins. All the toxic reactions or side effects ever reported, *total,* for all the vitamins used by millions of people in this country, for all the years that this agency has existed, are less than the toxic reactions and side effects reported *every year* for *each* of the ten drugs most commonly used in America." Biochemist Patrick Mooney, author of *Supernutrition* states that only one person in the past 25 years MAY have died from vitamin overdosing. On the other hand, drugs are potentially lethal. Misuse, and overdoses can and do kill people every day. In fact, some authorities place drugs as the third leading cause of death in America, second only to heart disease and cancer. Yet there has never been a single documented fatality or report of permanent damage or injury as a result of taking vitamin or mineral supplements!

## Vitamins and Minerals: How Much and When?

The best way to take vitamin and mineral supplements so that your body can utilize them effectively, is to take them in combination. Your vitamin supplement program should consist of everything from Vitamin A to the mineral zinc; everything in proper balance. Fortunately, our local health food stores now have products that have all the vitamins and minerals in combination, with the nutrients in proper balance, so that you don't have to read hundreds of books to figure it all out. Look at the label to see if the formula is complete, and also check the fillers if you are allergic to such things as lactose or corn, soya, wheat, or yeast. An excellent book on vitamin supplements is Earl Mindell's *Vitamin Bible.*

My daily regimen for optimum health begins with a high potency vitamin/mineral complex. I always check the B-complex first on the label, and look for at least 50 to 100 mgs of the B's. Additionally, I take 3,000 mgs of Vitamin C, because the amount of C in a multi-vitamin formula is usually very low. (Incidentally, people who work under fluorescent lights need extra C, because these lights deplete the body of approximately 45 mgs per hour. Also, smoking burns up approximately 25 mgs of C per cigarette). Vitamin E is also very important for health, and most multi-vitamins contain only about 50-100 I.U.'s of E. Vitamin E is an anti-oxidant, and is helpful for circulatory conditions, aging, and the heart. A well-researched book on this subject is *Vitamin E: Your Key to a Healthy Heart* by Herbert Bailey. Additionally, it has now been established that women need approximately 1,400 mgs of calcium a day, particularly after menopause, in order to avoid osteoporosis. Men need about 1,000 mgs of calcium daily. Calcium should always be taken in a calcium/magnesium formula, in a 2:1 ratio.

### Fiber

Fiber is absolutely necessary for health, and most people don't get enough of it. It is now known that lack of fiber is a contributory factor in colon and rectal cancers, the second most prevalent type of cancer in the country. Fiber helps soak up harmful substances in the food and in the intestines. Fiber keeps the entire gastrointestinal system functioning smoothly. In fact, if your diet is deficient in fiber, and this unfortunately applies to most of us, nothing you could do would restore your health faster than to correct this.

It is unwise to get all your fiber from bran alone. The best type of fiber is found in fruits and vegetables and is quite different from the crude fiber found in bran. For example, apple-pectin absorbs many different destructive materials from the intestinal tract. Certain fibers have a way of trapping and removing many harmful bacteria from the intestines. It binds a lot of the toxic agents that are produced in our bodies. Lewis Laboratories has a product entitled "Fabulous Fiber" made from fruits which is delicious tasting and comes in powder form.

### Smoking

No one needs to be told these days that smoking is bad for your health. We must recognize however, that there are a great many people who find it impossible to quit, even after paying enormous sums for stop-smoking courses, hypnosis, and other techniques. There are also those who find smoking pleasurable, and simply don't want to quit regardless of the possible health consequences. According to the U.S. Surgeon General's report in May, 1988, smoking is more addictive than heroin, and there are people who have quit for five, or even ten years, and find that one puff starts them right back again. While smokers need to be courteous and considerate around those not so addicted, non-smokers also need to have some understanding of the extent of this problem for those who are. Constantly badgering a smoker to quit seems to have a boomerang effect.

If you are in the category of those people who either refuse to quit, or find yourself unable to do so, then at least take some extra precautions to protect your lungs. The best advice on this comes from the excellent book by Durk Pearson and Sandy Shaw, *Life Extension*. Their research indicates that certain supplements (listed in their book) can help counteract the negative effects of smoking.

The above is a basic vitamin program for most people, but always check with your doctor first, preferably a nutritionally-oriented one. If you have special needs, such as dieting, taking drugs, or trying to slow down the aging process, consult some of the nutritional books listed in the bibliography.

## THE MAGIC POWER OF EXERCISE

Do not expect to be healthy all of your life if you are unwilling to exercise! Besides keeping our bodies healthy, exercise also improves our emotional well-being, keeps our mental capabilities sharp, works out tension, and can even help overcome such serious problems as depression. Any good aerobic routine (that means non-stop,) that speeds up the heart and breathing rates, done for a minimum of 30 minutes at a time, at least three times a week, will pay big, lifelong dividends.

Exercise gives you more energy; it relieves anxiety, it counteracts anger and hostility, it improves concentration and memory, it improves sleep, and it encourages a more positive self-image and improves self-confidence. People who exercise regularly feel better about themselves than people who don't. In fact, there seems to be a direct connection between physical activity and personal well-being and contentment.

A report from the national Center for Disease Control stated that, if you don't exercise regularly, you're endangering your heart almost as much as if you smoke. The CDC concluded from its studies that lack of exercise is as strong a risk for cardiovascular disease as smoking, high blood pressure, or high cholesterol, and stated that a sedentary lifestyle appears to be a greater threat to the health of American hearts than these other factors.

According to the American Cancer Society's analysis of more than one million people, reported at the July, 1987 conference in Seattle, researchers found that the overall death rate from cancer was lowest in those who exercised heavily, during work or play, and highest in those who never exercised. The data also indicated that moderate exercisers have significantly lower rates of lung, colorectal and pancreatic cancers.

Exercise also develops self-discipline. Psychiatrist Thaddeus Kostrubala, author of *The Joy of Running,* ,says that running works because it changes personality patterns. People develop a greater sense of their own value, They feel an increased sense of personal strength. And, growing evidence suggests that people who are aerobicaly fit may also have an edge intellectually. Researchers are convinced that exercise can improve concentration, creativity, and problem solving abilities. Twenty percent of the blood flow from the heart goes to the brain. During exercise when the heart is pumping hard, that blood flow is increased, and that means there's an increase in oxygen to the brain, helping us to think better. According to a study reported in *Prevention Magazine,* a test on elderly people, who often complain about memory lapses, showed that older people put on a 4-month brisk walking program improved in six out of eight mental ability tests, including reaction time and short-term memory. The sedentary control group showed no improvement.

A study on depression showed that jogging 5 days a week for a ten-week period was associated with significant reductions in depression scores. Among the depressed subjects who jogged, negative states of anger, hostility, fatigue, inertia, and anxiousness decreased. Positive states of cheerfulness and energy increased. In fact, in many cases depression is the result of a lifestyle of physical immobility. Inactivity is a form of self-abuse.

**Aging and Exercise**

There is no drug or potient in existence that holds as much promise for sustained health as regular exercise. It's the closest thing to an anti-aging pill. With age, the heart's ability to transport oxygen and nutrients via the blood steadily declines. But your heart will stay strong and efficient if you put it to use regularly through exercise. Numerous studies have shown that people in their sixties and seventies can become as fit and energetic as people thirty years younger simply by participating in a program of regular walking, swimming, jogging, or other forms of aerobic exercise. Getting older doesn't have to mean getting more tired. One of the greatest benefits of exercise is the additional energy people have when they become fit through exercise. But the body which is sedentary tires at the slightest effort. Some people complain that they're too tired to exercise. The truth is the reverse—they're tired because they don't exercise. Regular exercise gives one more vitality, stamina and energy by bringing more oxygen to the brain.

An article in the Canadian Journal of Public Health suggested that there is good evidence that regular exercise can be an effective agent in both retarding the aging process and in recovering lost vigor.

The physical degeneration which often accompanies aging may simply be the result of a sedentary lifestyle, and may be preventable. Older people with a high level of physical activity have better adaptability, higher vitality, increased physical capacity and improved resistance against illness, compared to physically inactive people, reported the Journal of Sports Medicine and Physical Fitness. Additionally, older people who are engaged in sports continuously since youth are biologically younger than untrained people of the same age. A longitudinal study of Harvard alumni published in 1986 found that those who exercise 3 to 5 hours a week lived an average of 2 years longer than those who didn't.

In order for exercise to improve the cardio-vascular system it must be continuous, uninterrupted, and steady. Stop-and-go exercise, such as tennis, golf, strenuous housework, or square dancing, simply do not bring about metabolic, cardiovascular and muscular changes. Nor do they contribute to weight loss. Only sustained, non-stop aerobic exercises put a demand on all the muscles of the body, including the heart muscle. But exercise doesn't have to be strenuous in order to be beneficial: you don't have to jog 10 miles every morning before breakfast. Brisk walking (3 to 4 miles per hour) is one of the most pleasant and beneficial exercises there is. A half-hour walk at a fast pace, done at least three times a week, will give you extra energy, drive calcium into the bones to prevent osteoporosis, improve your cardiovascular system, muscle strength and flexibility, improve your mental well-being, help you keep a trim figure, and improve posture.

Just as you cannot be in optimum health without proper nutrition, so too you cannot be totally healthy unless you are willing to exercise at least three times a week, preferably five, for a minimum of 20 minutes; preferably thirty. Every muscle in the body should be exercised every single day. It's because we fail to do this that we suffer so many little aches and pains. Many headaches, backaches, constipation, arthritic-type pains, and so forth could be completely eliminated simply by getting ourselves on a program of regular exercise. And—it could even be a lot of fun!

**Stress Reduction**

In the tense world in which we live, nothing is more important than learning how to relax. When we take a little time out each day to let go and relax, the endless onslaught of worried thoughts and images is replaced by a quiet, peaceful state which brings health to the body and mind. The multiple sources of stress in modern life create prolonged tension, and this impacts our health, happiness and productivity. The most frequent problem the average doctor sees today is chronic fatigue, which no pill can cure, but it can be alleviated by taking the time to stop for a moment, breathe deeply, and release the tension from one's muscles, thereby allowing more energy to flow to the brain.

The payoffs to the person skilled in relaxation are great indeed. With skill in muscle relaxation a person can improve their physical health, learn faster, conquer anxiety, work more efficiently, cope with stress, enjoy more harmonious interpersonal relationships, and discover more joy in life.

Tension is muscular tightness. Muscles in the forehead, neck, shoulders, abdomen, or other areas tighten up and stay tense when one is in a conflict situation, or in a demanding job. Eventually those muscles begin to ache from being too tense too long, and one then discovers a tension headache, a pain in the neck, or backache. A person is usually not aware of persisting muscle tension because s/he slowly gets used to it and comes to accept it as something that is to be expected. He is simply unaware that muscles are more tense than is required for the work they are doing. A person who has learned to relax, however, can also learn to become aware of mounting tension before it causes a headache or other pain. By attending to his muscles, he can talk to them and tell them to relax and let go.

Although it may sound contradictory, the skill of relaxation actually increases energy. This is because tension inhibits muscle resiliency, and vital energy is wasted. Relaxed muscles, on the other hand, are conserving energy and they also stand ready to move when necessary. Relaxed voluntary muscles also lead to relaxation for the rest of the body, including involuntary functions. Ductless glands stop secreting stimulants into the blood and the digestive system slows its churning. The heart eases its strained pumping against constricted blood vessels. The blood pathways, in turn, open to let life-giving blood flow easily throughout the body. A person skilled in relaxation is a vibrantly energetic person whose energy springs from a relaxed, healthy body.

Chronic tension affects learning and emotions too. A tense person cannot learn difficult concepts or solve complex problems as well. The more tense she is, the less able she is to master the material and grasp concepts. Her emotional responses are often exaggerated and irritable. On the other hand, the skilled relaxor can work long hours, and sleep deeply and soundly. She discovers an enlarged capacity for learning and memory, and is vibrantly energetic and alert. And she usually enjoys warm interpersonal relationships.

A study with a group of 42 hypertensive patients compared the effects of no treatment with a program of progressive muscle relaxation over a period of 8 weeks. The results support the findings from other investigations that relaxation training results in decreases in resting systolic and/or diastolic blood pressure in patients with essential hypertension. (Archives of General Psychiatry, June, 1982).

One of the best ways to learn to relax is through practicing meditation, which was discussed in Chapter 8. Two good books on this subject are *The Relaxation Response,* by Dr. Herbert Benson, and *A Guide to Stress Reduction,* by L. John Mason, Ph.D.

Health is a positive state of wellness, available to the person who takes responsibility for his or her own health. The medical crisis in this country will end when people take responsibility for their illnesses, and realize that what causes most sickness is the way they are living their lives.

Dr. Blair Justice says: "By examining our attitudes toward illness, and toward our life, we may discover how we disease ourselves and, subsequently, how we may recover the ability to help ourselves in the healing process."

The body expresses that which we are—it is an instrument for the expression of the soul. It is a representation of the thoughts which we have selected. "The gods we worship write their names on our faces." If you will choose predominantly positive emotions, eat properly, and exercise daily, you need never be sick. —Think of the money you'll save, in addition to the happiness you will experience from having a strong, healthy, energetic body all of your life!

# ten

# SELF-HEALING
# THROUGH VISUALIZATION

> *Thoughts and mental images are capable of*
> *initiating physiologic changes in your body.*
> *You can control your own thoughts;*
> *you can heal yourself*
> *just as you learned to make your body walk.*
> *The key is to picture your body normalized.*
> *—Dr. Irving Oyle*
> *The Healing Mind*

The human body, unlike a machine, has the ability to heal itself; and the healing power is under the control of your mind, which can cause disease or create health. The great majority of diseases are psychosomatic, meaning that the origin is in the mind, and the result is in the body. So, if we can be psychosomatically ill, why can't we be psychosomatically healthy?

If, through stress or negative thinking, you have created a *dis-ease* in your body, you can also create the conditions which will allow the healing process to occur. Most disease is caused by incorrect thinking patterns, radiating their negative energy within the body. If you change these unhealthy beliefs and emotions, you can literally rebuild your body by rebuilding your thinking. The amazing fact about the body is that you already have healing power within you which is far more powerful than any form of external treatment! The most advanced medications available to doctors today can only approximate what the body itself produces, which is a built-in apothecary, without the disadvantages of the toxicity of drugs.

Dr. Franz Inglefinger, the former editor of the prestigious New England Journal of Medicine, stated that 85 percent of all people who bring complaints and symptoms to their physicians are suffering from self-limiting disorders. Meaning that, more than four times out of five, what ails you is well within the reach of the body's own healing mechanisms. Contrary to popular belief, doctors really don't heal anything; it's always our internal mechanism that does the healing.

133

The physician merely helps suppress the symptoms by giving you a drug so that you won't be as aware of your discomfort until the body has a chance to heal itself. But, of course, every drug is toxic and has some side effect; in fact some drugs are very poisonous, so it is always wiser to facilitate the healing by natural means, instead of suppressing the symptom by medicating it.

A disease is not merely a physical problem, isolated in the body, but it is a problem of the whole person. Our emotions play a significant role not only in susceptibility to disease, but in recovery. Illness is a symptom of problems elsewhere in an individual's life. Mind and body are one inseparable system; whatever affects the mind affects the body, and the converse is also true. Every thought we think, no matter how innocuous, has an immediate physiological effect: everything a person thinks and feels and believes is experienced directly in the body. Thus, if we consciously change our thoughts to those which are healthy, joyful, and loving, we will radiate these feelings within our bodies and can produce the corresponding effect. If we realize that we play a part in creating our own illnesses through our thoughts and emotions, then we can recognize that we can play a part in creating our own health, and it has now been confirmed that a person's mental attitude can help or hinder the body's self-healing mechanism.

Dr. Lawrence LeShan, psychologist and author of several books on the mind's role in health and disease, including *You Can Save Your Life,* and *The Medium, The Mystic, and The Physicist,* has this to say on the subject:

*The mind has untapped potential far beyond the everyday uses that we make of it.*

*Self-healing is a major factor in curing most illnesses.*

*A patient's mental attitude can help or hinder the body's self-healing mechanisms.*

*Through various forms of meditation, the power of the mind or psyche can be enlisted for the purpose of speeding up the healing process.*

At a conference organized by the Institute for the advancement of Health in New York in 1985, researcher Brendan O'Regan said: "If negative emotions tend to have negative consequences, a complementary science may exist. Positive emotions, as author Norman Cousins once pointed out, act as a buffer or block, like analgesia. They are a bullet-proof vest that protects the body and enables it to get on with its main job—living." Reports from Stanford University correlate laughter with rises in adrenaline, noradrenaline and dopamine. Shifting emotional states can now be correlated with shifting hormones. James Henry of Loma Linda University found that changing feelings from security to helplessness were accompanied by

134

rising blood levels of adrenal corticoids. Taken together, these findings show a pattern, O'Regan said. "Over time negative emot..ons can bring about negative body states, which may be stepping stones to disease. Positive emotions may prevent illness by offsetting the damaging consequences of negative emotions.

Years ago, in a Concept-Therapy class, I met Glenda, a fifty-five year old woman whose hands were so crippled with arthritis that she could not dress herself or comb her hair. Six months later, she had completely arrested the arthritis, felt no pain and her hands were totally mobile. How could this be? Glenda learned the principles of mental healing which will be described in this chapter. She began talking to her hands daily and specifically directing the calcium deposits in the joints of her fingers to break down and be eliminated through her body in a normal fashion. She came to realize that there is *consciousness* in every molecule of matter, even in the abnormal growth in her hands. More importantly, this consciousness can be contacted and directed when we understand its laws, and it will do our bidding when we approach it correctly.

**The New Synthesis**

Now that we have discussed the mind's role in the creation of disease, let us examine the part our thinking can play in creating health. In the past decade, there has been a quiet revolution in the medical field which has resulted in the establishment of new institutes for healing, called holistic health centers. These are staffed not only by medical doctors, but also by practitioners of acupuncture, hypnosis, psychology, homeopathy, chiropractic, naturopathy, and nutritional therapists who recognize the contribution vitamins and minerals can play in the maintenance of health. Mind control, such as using mental imagery in healing, positive affirmations, and meditation and relaxation techniques are also being taught to promote well-being. In the last decade, there has been a synthesis of ancient and modern techniques, such as traditional medicine and metaphysics, Zen Buddhism and quantum physics. The archaic mind/body dualism of Descartes has been replaced by the knowledge that mind and body are unified and, whatever affects a part affects the whole. When body and mind function together in harmony, health exists. Illness results when stress and conflict disrupt this process. Out of this understanding emerges the freedom of each individual to participate actively in creating and sustaining the health of his or her body.

135

## Healing Through Imagery

Simonton and the staff of his clinic in Texas, are realizing remarkable success in utilizing visual imagery in their treatment program for terminal cancer patients, and have described the technique in their excellent book *Getting Well Again*. When Simonton was the chief radiation oncologist at Travis Air Force Base in California, he used the technique with an aviator whose advanced throat cancer portended certain death. The cancer had reached the size of a peach, and was occluding the openings to the lungs and stomach, and spreading rapidly.

Simonton taught the patient a procedure of deep muscular relaxation through which he could enter the alpha state where the brain waves are slowed down from normal activity, so that he was closer to his subconscious mind. He was then told to visualize his cancer in some way, and to fantasize that the malignant cells were being destroyed.

The patient began to visualize his white blood cells (part of the body's immune system) as riders on horseback. They began attacking and destroying the cancer cells. This image was repeated for fifteen minutes three times a day, and over a period of seven weeks the tumor receded in size and finally disappeared. At the end of this time the patient's biopsy specimens revealed only normal tissue.

Simonton and Matthews believe that stress and depression are two negative attitudes that can prevent cancer cures or cause a person to develop cancer. Simonton states:

*I'm convinced a patient's attitude plays a vital role as to whether or not he will recover from cancer, even in terminal cases. What's more, a negative psychological attitude can make a person more susceptible to getting cancer. A person who believes he will die as a result of his cancer, or that he is going to develop cancer, will usually have his expectation fulfilled. On the other hand, when these negative attitudes are changed to positive ones, the results are often amazing.*

*If we are going to believe that we have the power in our own minds to overcome cancer, then we have to admit that we also have the power to bring on the disease in the first place. With those patients who are willing to stay with us and persist, we invariably find that the cancer has filled some emotional need.*

Simonton's technique for assisting cancer patients to heal themselves can be used with slight modification in the treatment of any disease. Here are the basic steps:

1.  *Get into a comfortable position and relax yourself deeply.*
2.  *For about two minutes, picture a pleasant scene, such as walking through the woods on a summer day, strolling along the beach, or sailing on the bay.*

3.    *Visualize how you think your disease looks. (It doesn't need to be exact. Most of us are sufficiently in touch with our bodies to produce at least a vague idea of what is happening within it.)*

4.    *Picture your immunity mechanism in some fashion: the white blood cells going in and carrying out the dead, destroyed cells and eliminating them through the urine and bowels. See your white cells as very strong, very aggressive, attacking the cancer cells and destroying them. See the cancer shrinking, the liver and kidneys taking it out of the body with the urine and stool. See yourself beginning to feel better, becoming more in tune with life, having more energy, a better appetite, more pleasant relationships. Frequently, during the day, affirm: MY BODY HAS THE ABILITY TO REPAIR ITSELF, AND IT IS DOING SO NOW!*

5.    *Repeat this procedure three times a day for fifteen minutes each session. If done faithfully and with confidence, at the end of approximately twenty-one days you will notice a remarkable change!*

Mental healing does not, of course, preclude medical assistance. It should be viewed as an adjunct to whatever traditional methods you are now utilizing.

One beautiful spring afternoon a few years ago I received a telephone call from a distraught client who said she had accidentally amputated almost half of her right index finger while trying to repair the chain on an exercise bicycle. She was rushed to a hospital carrying the amputated portion in a saline solution. Initially, the doctor declined to graft the severed piece to the remainder of her finger, stating that it was hopeless. Finally, after realizing how distressed Dot was, the physician said he would suture the amputated portion on only as a "biological dressing," because the odds of saving the finger were less then a hundred to one.

Of all the people who have come to me for counseling, Dot was one of the most obdurately skeptical. A super-intelligent, multi-talented woman who relied completely on her intellect to deal with life, she had no awareness at the time of metaphysics or self-healing techniques. Nevertheless, I encouraged her to believe she could heal her finger by utilizing the considerable power of her subconscious mind. I instructed her in the techniques of visualization and affirmations, and she began repeating the following affirmations aloud four times each day:

*Every day, my finger is becoming more and more whole.*
*The graft is taking, and the parts are now joining*
*more and more firmly and completely.*
*My finger is becoming healthier and healthier*
*and is healing rapidly.*
*The nail is being restored*
*through growth of a new healthy one.*
*Thank you Spirit within every cell of my body,*
*for effecting this healing.*

In addition, twice a day for fifteen minutes each time, she diligently relaxed completely in a comfortable chair, put herself into a state of self-hypnosis, and visualized her finger totally healed and perfectly normal in every way. She also increased her daily regimen of vitamins, particularly taking large dosages of Vitamin C to help strengthen her body's immune system while the healing was taking place. Dot was also more careful about eating healthy, nutritious foods during this period, and was scrupulous about following her doctor's instructions to keep the wound clean with frequent changes of the dressing. And, she supplemented her doctor's suggestions and her own healing concepts by listening twice a day to a self-healing tape I made especially for her.

Ten days after the suturing, Dot encountered a new doctor in the outpatient clinic who insisted that the amputated portion, which had blackened, was necrotic, (dead), and must be removed. She was told that she would not be allowed to leave the hospital until that surgery was performed because of the likelihood of gangrene spreading down her arm. When Dot begged for "just a little more time," two other physicians were consulted; and one of them agreed that she could retain the graft a little longer. Six days after this she was again told that the amputated portion was indeed dead. But, at Dot's insistence, the doctor again permitted her to retain the graft. Twenty-six days after the accident the doctor finally acknowledged that the finger, with its graft, was healing and stated: "I don't know what you're doing, but keep doing it!" At the end of two more months her finger was completely healed and appears perfectly normal.

Recently, the medical establishment has permitted students in nursing and medical schools to experiment with mental healing as a part of their professional training. "The doors are opening because there is factual evidence for unconventional healing, and you can't argue with facts," says psychologist Evelyn Monahan, who teaches a course on "The Power and Use of the Mind" to students at Emory University's School of Nursing in Atlanta, Georgia. In her course, Dr. Monahan instructs nurses in how to use telepathy to reach comatose patients, and to use clairvoyance to pick up subliminal leads in analyzing medical histories; plus her specialty, psychic healing.

"You can use the mind to affect external things, including the molecular structure of the body," Dr. Monahan believes. And one of the most effective techniques, she feels, is visualization. "I teach the nurses to actually *see* diseased organs or infections of the body repairing themselves," she explains. "If you want to fight infection, you can visualize the white blood cells speeding to the site of the infection and destroying the invading body."

Dr. Irving Oyle, author of *The Healing Mind,* is another pioneer in the use of visualization, meditation, and affirmations in self-healing. He states that:

> *By changing the consciousness, the mental picture you have of what's going on in your body, you can change the physical body, according to this new emerging medical model. By thinking themselves sick, people become sick. We know, for instance, that there is an ulcer-type personality, which is prone to thinking itself into ulcers. There is a certain type of personality that tends to get heart attacks. If you can think yourself into them, why can't you think yourself out of them? And, if you change the thinking pattern or the visual imagery to restore health, you become your own healer.*

## The Law of Vibration

Healing yourself or another comes under the law of vibration. A vibration can be transmitted from one person to another through the medium of the resonant electric waves of the brain cells of the sender to the brain cells of the receiver. This has been demonstrated repeatedly through the phenomenon of mental telepathy.

Disease is just a vibration, and so is health; the former being the lower frequency and health the high. All sickness is nothing but a maladjustment of frequencies, and all we have to do to effect a healing is to change the frequency. The individual consciousness of the various organs of the body each have their individual frequencies since all consciousness has its degree-frequency. Spirit, which is present within every cell of a patient's body, can be consciously contacted and directed through utilizing the law of vibration properly.

DISEASE ⟋⟍⟍⟍⟍⟍⟍⟍⟍⟍⟍⟍⟍⟍ HEALTH

When a drug is given to a sick person and it helps to effect a healing, all that has happened is that the particular chemical, which vibrates at a certain frequency, has interacted with the patient's frequency to bring it closer to normal. Every drug has its own frequency which can stimulate the vibration of a patient's organs. Digitalis, for example, is used to stimulate the vibration of the heart, and thereby it changes its frequency. In the same manner, concentrated thought force can increase, stimulate, and restore the patient's overall frequency to produce a condition of perfectly normal functioning. It's the same principle used in a different way; but it doesn't have any side effects!

If you change the vibration of something, you change its form; you change its condition. In order to change a vibration, we must apply energy and, in mental healing, it is energy in the form of thought. For example, on the physical plane, one can change ice into water by applying energy in the form of heat, and we have actually changed its form by speeding up its vibration. Then we can take that same water and apply energy to it, which means to step up its vibration further, and it will become steam. Here again, by changing the vibration, we have changed the form.

It is the same principle in relationship to changing disease into health. If you apply energy in the form of your concentrated thought vibrations, you will change the form or condition from one of illness to one of health.

To change a person's vibration on a conscious level, we must first establish a condition of resonance or rapport with that person in order for our suggestion to lodge in his or her subconscious mind. When two minds are in harmony with each other, clairvoyance and the transmission of thought are possible. Do not attempt to give a healing suggestion to someone who will scoff at you because the suggestion will not penetrate his or her subconscious mind. In such cases, send them healing thoughts when you are away from them because this bypasses the conscious mind.

In conditions of semiconsciousness, or unconsciousness, the suggestions should be given aloud because they will be directly received by the subconscious. When people are in a coma, under anesthesia, in a state of shock after an accident, having a seizure, or sleeping, their subconscious minds are wide open; and anything that is said in their presence will be accepted by Spirit Within them, which will begin carrying it out. In these cases you contact Spirit directly, without intervention from the conscious reasoning mind, and it is always Spirit that does the healing, no matter what the method is—pill, shot, surgery, chiropractic adjustment, traction—or whatever. Always remember that *you* have no power to heal, but you can be an instrument for Spirit to effect a change in the body of the afflicted person. All you have to do to help a person is to give positive, constructive healing concepts to Spirit, and It will do the work. Remember, the Power that made the body can heal the body!

Just as you can give a person a healing concept if you are with him or her, so can you perform absent healing if the ill person is not present. If you know someone who is ill and you apply energy in the form of your thought waves, imagining that person well and happy, then you can change the condition by raising his or her vibrations, provided you put sufficient concentration behind it.

A woman who attended one of my seminars at the University of Santa Clara in California, was scheduled for an operation in two weeks to have a tumor removed from her uterus. Sandy told me about it, and I suggested it would be worthwhile to try imagery first to see if surgery could be avoided. We organized a healing group of five people and, at separate locations at the predesignated time of 9 p.m., each one of us spent ten minutes sending healing energy to Sandy and concentrating on seeing her healthy and happy. At the end of twelve days Sandy was reexamined by her doctor who told her that he could not find any evidence of the tumor, and the operation was postponed.

During the same time period, another student told me he was to have a prostate gland operation and was very concerned about it. That evening I went to a study group meeting where twenty people were present and asked everyone to join me in an image for this man's health. Because of the personal nature of the problem, I didn't describe it to the group, but led an image in which we visualized him smiling, healthy, and active. A few days later he was feeling so good that he checked with his doctor again who decided that he could postpone the operation. To this day, ten years later, he has never had to have it.

Absent healing, either with a group or alone, can be very effective. On the following page is a description of the technique which you can utilize whenever necessary. Of course, if an individual has become ill through repeated indulgence in negative emotions, such as anger, depression, or fear, then mental healing will only be effective for a limited period of time; for the simple reason that the person will once again make himself or herself dis-eased through disturbed emotions. The same thing applies, of course, to traditional medical means of healing: the cure is only temporary if the individual does not change his/her life style and thinking process. Either the illness will reappear or symptom substitution will occur. Thus, healing is a matter of the entire psyche, not just the physical body.

An additional mental healing technique, used down through the ages by psychics and spiritual healers, is to visualize a beautiful white light cascading over the head, shoulders, and body of the afflicted individual. See this pure, brilliant, healing light penetrating deeply into every cell and pore of the body, cleansing and purifying it, and bringing the body up to a level of perfectly normal functioning. It is an effective technique for use in all mental healing, and it is said by metaphysicians that this "thought form" is actually created around the person on the astral plane.

141

# HEALING IMAGE

1.     Prearrange with the sick person, and with others who have agreed to participate, the time you are going to make your image. (9 p.m. is preferred.)

2.     A few moments before the designated time, go into a room where you may be alone for ten minutes, turn out the lights, seat yourself in a comfortable chair, relax yourself, and begin to VISUALIZE the sick person sitting in his or her chair or bed, in a passive, receptive state of mind. Their Innate Mind is as open as possible to receive the curative image.

3.     As you picture this person sitting there, say the following aloud:

**Spirit Within is healing you now.**
**Every day, in every respect,**
**you are becoming healthier and healthier.**

4.     Repeat this over and over, in a sing-song tone of voice. Do not use your will, but use your imagination when you repeat the affirmation, and strongly VISUALIZE the person looking and acting completely healthy in every way.

5.     Feel that the person's subconscious mind is receiving your message, and concentrate as much as possible on sending your thoughts to them. Imagine that the person is surrounded by a White Healing Light that is pouring down and through their whole body, penetrating deeply into every cell, nerve and fiber, bringing the entire vibration of their body up to a state of PERFECTLY NORMAL FUNCTIONING, whatever is normal for that particular individual. SEE this light penetrating deeply into their body, and see the person smiling, healthy and happy.

6.     At the end of ten minutes, turn the image over to Spirit to carry it out in the person's body. Then, break your concentration and leave the room.

7.     Do not try to reach the subconscious mind unless you put your heart into this. Put all your concentration into the idea of Perfect Health, and try not to think of anything else while you are in the room. If you do, Spirit will receive the message and act upon it, and the sick person will be forever grateful to you for using your energies to help life. The Law of Cause and Effect will then operate in **your** life to keep you in perfect health.

142

Dr. Fleet says:

*That Power which we call the Divine working through our bodies, if It gets the order through our wrong thinking to build a cancer, will build a perfect cancer.*

*Consider the lowly spider without an educated brain. This Power works through the spider and it weaves its web of the most delicate material, and of the most intricate geometrical designs that our architects consider to be a marvel.*

*Man must take responsibility for the state of his body, for we are the product of our thought creations. Whatever condition our body is in, and whatever the state of our mind, is a replication of what we have selected from the thought plane, manifesting in our life. Every illness in your or my body is a direct result of some image in our mental life. We say we have bad luck, but there is no such thing as bad luck or chance in this universe of Cause and Effect.*

*When a person knows this, and properly understands it, s/he will naturally begin to image correctly. Instead of violating this Law of Creation and worrying about the things he does not want, he will begin to visualize and image and fashion and plan that which he does want, and he or she will have a new world, and all of our disease-ridden bodies will be replaced by healthy ones.*

The primary fact we must become increasingly aware of is that thoughts and mental images are capable of initiating physiological changes in our bodies. We can learn to control our thoughts and direct positive energy to ourselves and others, and thus become an active participant in the creation and maintenance of our own health. Remember, thought is *creative,* and your own thinking processes can bring you total health, energy, stamina and aliveness!

> *We are in midst*
> *of as dramatic a*
> *transformation as has*
> *ever occurred in science.*
> *—Blair Justice*

Here is a useful diagram for pinpointing your stress throughout the day. You can cut this out and refer to it frequently during the day. Simply estimate where the hands of your clock are at the particular moment and, if they are climbing up the tension side, close your eyes for a moment, do the deep breathing exercise, and see if you can get both hands back down to six o'clock.

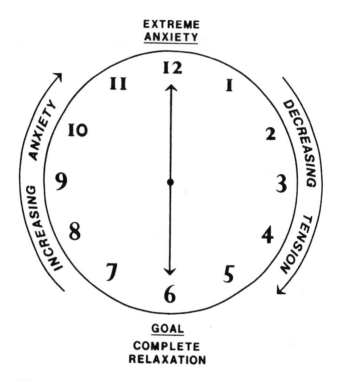

EXTREME
ANXIETY

GOAL
COMPLETE
RELAXATION

### Conditioning Relaxation Process

*PINPOINT WHERE THE HANDS OF YOUR INTERNAL CLOCK ARE AT THE MOMENT. THE OBJECTIVE IS TO GET BOTH HANDS DOWN TO 6 O'CLOCK.*

1. Exhale forcefully.

2. Breathe in deeply through your nose to the count of 6.

3. Breathe out SLOWLY through your mouth to the count of 6.

Each time you inhale and exhale you will feel twice as comfortable as you did before.

144

# eleven
# COSMIC CONSCIOUSNESS: THE ULTIMATE GOAL

*There is a mental state*
*so happy, so glorious,*
*that all the rest of life*
*is worthless compared to it...*
—*Richard Maurice Bucke, M.D.*
*Cosmic Consciousness*

In the earlier chapters of this book we discussed how Spirit has progressively evolved Itself through the electronic, mineral, plant, and animal phases, and then to man. And it appears that It still has one more phase of development before It finally merges back into Itself, the All. This sixth phase is termed the Cosmic, or Divine, phase of creation. We know that this phase exists because we have had individuals in the history of the world who entered consciously into it while they lived on earth, and they left the record of their lives and deeds as a model for man to aspire towards. These cosmically conscious men and women were living in a state of awareness that was far advanced over those of the ordinary people we deal with in our everyday existence, those who are locked into the human phase and cannot conceive of anything beyond the material world of possessions.

Cosmic consciousness means *the state of awareness or knowledge one has when he or she becomes consciously aware of the organization of the universe, and of his or her oneness with it.* Furthermore, such a person will translate this knowledge into a living experience.

The diagram on the next page illustrates that there are three forms or levels, of consciousness: simple, self, and cosmic, and we can symbolically place everything that exists on this continuum. The first section represents the lowest forms of life with just simple consciousness—from inorganic matter to the least evolved human being, primitive man. The second portion begins with primitive man and ends with the highest type of individual, such as Albert Schweitzer or Plato. The third portion represents the lowest type of cosmic consciousness on up to the fully developed divine awareness typifying the perfect human being.

0%
100%

SIMPLE
(Plant and animal)

SELF
(Human)

COSMIC
(Divine)

CONTINUUM OF CONSCIOUSNESS

146

Everyone is situated somewhere on this scale of consciousness and, just as in the human realm, we have many degrees of human awareness, so also in the cosmic. Down through the ages there have been a number of individuals who have developed this power of transcendent realization, and some of them have been chronologued in a very interesting book by Dr. Maurice Bucke entitled *Cosmic Consciousness*. The people he discusses in this book obviously don't represent all the people who have ever had an illumination, as it was written in 1901, but it provides an extensive history of the Illuminata of the race. In his definitive work Dr. Bucke delineates the characteristics of the cosmic-conscious person, and explores the lives of people, such as Spinoza, Emerson, Walt Whitman, Dante, Buddha, and Christ, that he determined, according to his criteria, had the cosmic sense to a greater or lesser degree.

Dr. Bucke says:

*The prime characteristic of cosmic consciousness is a consciousness of the cosmos, that is, of the life and order of the universe. With self-consciousness one is concerned mainly with oneself. With cosmic consciousness one extends his perception to the entire universe. Along with the consciousness of the cosmos there occurs an intellectual enlightenment or illumination which alone would place the individual on a new plane of existence—would make him almost a member of a new species.*

*There exists a family sprung from, living among, but scarcely forming a part of ordinary humanity, whose members are spread abroad throughout the advanced races of mankind, and throughout the last forty centuries of the world's history. The trait that distinguishes these people from others is this: their spiritual eyes have been opened and they have seen. These people dominate the last 25 centuries as stars of the first magnitude dominate the midnight sky. A person is identified as a member of this family by the fact that, at a certain age, he has passed through a new birth and risen to a higher spiritual plane.*

Of course, this does not mean that, when a person has cosmic consciousness, s/he knows everything about the universe. We all realize that, at about three years of age, when we acquired *self*-consciousness, we did not automatically know everything about ourselves; on the contrary, after a great many thousands of years of experience the members of the human race still know comparatively little about themselves. So, neither does a person know all about the cosmos merely because s/he has an illumination, but that individual does have a vastly increased awareness over the merely self-conscious person. Just as there are varying degrees of human consciousness, so also in the cosmic. This fact accounts for the differences in reports on the nature of the universe by those who have achieved cosmic consciousness; such as Christ, Buddha, and Socrates. Although all contain the central truths which are nearly always identical, there are variations in their perception and reporting of these principles.

Dr. Thurman Fleet, founder of Concept-Therapy states:

*The spiritual life is the highest expression of Spirit Within, exemplified by such attributes of character as love, generosity, aspiration, kindness, and so forth...Very few mortals have attained to the highest form of consciousness, that of the cosmic, and usually when they do such individuals are hailed as saviors of the world. When we fully realize the meaning of these terms and the mysteries they represent, we discover that, while it may have been the special mission of one, such as Christ, or Buddha, to undertake the work of enlightening a particular age, there are many other Masters or Illuminated souls engaged in other work, both on this plane, and on many other planes of existence, who are interested in helping to advance the consciousness of the world.*

In order to move into the Divine or Cosmic Phase, one must develop and learn to rely on the faculty of intuition instead of the much poorer tool, reason. Intuition is the chief characteristic of the cosmic individual. We must become increasingly aware of the inner world and constantly tune our consciousness into it. What we are seeking is *habitual spiritual consciousness,* not Sunday morning spiritual consciousness that throws a dollar into the collection plate and then forgets about it for the rest of the week, but a constant awareness of our oneness with all of life. Intuition can be cultivated, but the bargain intuition drives is that it will serve you, if you serve it. We must train this latent faculty and learn to obey it in order to retain the use of it. As discussed in Chapter 5, one of the primary ways to develop our intuition is through meditation.

Dr. Bucke states:

*The immediate future of our race is indescribably hopeful. The germ of cosmic consciousness has been planted in many individuals and, as this germ grows, more and more people will come into an understanding of this higher state until finally the majority of the race will have some degree of the cosmic knowledge. Then the human soul will be revolutionized... Men and women will know that God is within them, that the world is ruled by immutable laws, and by knowing the laws they will know that it is beneficial to obey them. Each act performed will be an act for the Divine, each day lived will be a day dedicated to the Divine...Each soul, through imparted knowledge, will know and feel itself to be immortal and will know that the entire universe with all its good exists for, and belongs to it, forever. Each person will come to know that violation of spiritual laws does not pay, and each will begin to pattern his or her life according to the real, and peace and happiness will be abundant everywhere.*

Cosmic consciousness comes to the person who learns, and lives by, the higher spiritual principles which govern life. Merely knowing about the cosmological laws but not living by them will not place a person into higher consciousness; he or she must become one with the cosmic by obeying the laws involved.

A person may have a very great desire to attain cosmic consciousness but, if the will power is weak, they will accomplish nothing. The will can be trained, and it *must* be trained over and over again until, by a natural habit, it will do the bidding of the higher self. One of the most important factors in this accomplishment is earnestness. When a person is a disciple of the higher path, he or she must be resolute about the quest. The word *disciple* comes from 'discipline,'' which means training of the mind or character. Until the will has been sufficiently trained and developed, all progress is rendered utterly impossible. Yet how few take the time to develop the will. How few develop their mind. Most people are just too lazy; they would rather watch T.V. or be entertained by someone else than put their own brain cells to work. Some people want the secrets, but they don't want to give up their negative way of living. This is an impossible demand. To such a one as this, the higher knowledge will never be obtained.

The moving account which history affords us of Buddha in the wilderness, spending six long years in mortification and meditation trying to achieve enlightenment, stands as a monumental record of one man's personal dedication to a vision. Buddha himself said there were many times during that long wait when he was ''almost overcome by the terrors of the dark forest'' and the austerities which he had imposed upon himself. When people seek enlightenment with such singlemindedness, they are sure to get it. Many people express a desire for cosmic consciousness, but how many are willing to exert the enormous courage of a Buddha as he faced the fears and trials of his lonely vigil?

We must also realize that Spirit is limited by the medium through which It expresses Itself. For instance, It is much more limited in Its expression through a little bird than through a human being. The Great Power that fills the universe is in and of Itself perfect, but its expression through our medium depends upon the condition of that medium. A good analogy is that of beautiful music being played by a large symphony orchestra in an acoustically perfect music hall, which is then recorded and transmitted by a radio broadcasting station and received by numerous stereo sets in the area. Some of these sets are in excellent condition with speakers and amplifiers having sufficient capacity and quality to express the music perfectly. In others, the receiving equipment is imperfect and, as a consequence, the same beautiful music is expressed imperfectly. So it is with man. The Great Power which fills the universe is perfect in Itself, but Its expression through our particular form depends upon the condition of that medium. Through constantly learning to contact our inner self we can get our life in tune with the Great Conductor of the Universe, thereby becoming a perfect expression of that Infinite Power. And this is our task as human beings.

In the Concept-Therapy text, Dr. Fleet states that:

*There seems to come a time for all of us when we become weary of pursuing outer sensations, and our attention reverts to the world within. Trying to figure out a solution to the problems of life, we become seekers after truth. Our consciousness is then led inward; and if we persist in our journey, we finally become aware of the orderly arrangement of the universe. We become cognizant of a great, all-pervading Power which rules everything and, as we progress, we try to learn more about it. No longer does the material world absorb all our attention. Something new has come into our lives: a desire to know about the inner or spiritual world. We then enter the path leading to cosmic consciousness.*

*New life seems to come: our vitality is rejuvenated; we eagerly absorb all that we can. We study, we meditate; and in our studying and meditation we find, here and there, a bit of truth. These bits we hoard and treasure until we have many which we attempt to put together, like a child working with a jigsaw puzzle. At long last one great truth dawns upon us: the world and everything in it is governed and operates by laws—great cosmological principles.*

*Now we ask: what are those laws? We go here, there, seeking, seeking. This quest goes on and on. If we persist in our struggle for an answer, sifting through the heterogenous*

150

*maze of philosophies, religions, treatises, we will find that*
*which we have long sought, the truth of the cosmic*
*organization. We take a firm hold on the Eternal Principles*
*of Natural Law and, as we learn them, we become conscious*
*of something new having entered our lives: an awareness of*
*the One. We are now truly on the Path of Attainment, having*
*entered a higher state of consciousness, that of the cosmic.*

This, then, is the goal of man, the goal towards which we are all striving, whether or not we are aware of it. Spiritual men and women are "the saviors of the world," and the spiritual person is also the creative one. By definition, a spiritual person is, to a high degree, united with the Divine aspect of his or her being; and that individual's life and thoughts proceed from the spiritual realm, thus bringing a creative life into the world that is not dictated by the lives of others: it is an original creation. The truly spiritual person always changes the world in some way. Nearly all of the good, the inspiration, and the uplifting thoughts of this world have been produced by the spirit of idealists, such as Plato, Kant, Albert Schweitzer, Spinoza, and poetic souls like Walt Whitman.

Only when we are grounded in the certainty that we are a manifestation of the Divine Consciousness within our physical form do we cease to feel lost and alone. It is the experience of the Infinite which enables us to break through the isolation, anxiety, and estrangement of self-conscious existence. Spirit is all-pervasive in the universe, and we are totally dependent upon this Consciousness for our existence. In the certainty of the knowledge of the omnipresent Spirit, we have achieved inner peace. God is not a patriarchal being but, for lack of a better word, an Energy Force which our limited, finite consciousness is powerless to comprehend or conceptualize. Yet the conscious awareness that everything and everyone *is* Its existence means that we are in a holy place even when we are in the most worldly place, for everything is rooted in the Divine Life. In the words of the great theologian Paul Tillich: "If one always experienced the Divine Presence, there would be no difference between the sacred and the secular, because this difference does not exist in the Divine Consciousness."

When a person fully understands the real meaning of the fact that s/he is a radiant expression of the Divine Spirit in manifestation, his or her behavior is always governed by that one central concept. A person's religion is not what they claim to believe in; it is what they do with their lives. What are their ultimate concerns? To what have they dedicated their lives and thoughts and actions? That is their true religion. Socrates taught that a person who really understands the truth and the idea of the good can never act against that idea. That person's entire existential relationship to life will be motivated, governed, and directed by his inner, existential relationship to the Divine; thus, it would be impossible to be unfaithful to that illuminated understanding.

Having outlined the task that lies before us, how shall we attain this goal? Naturally, it will not be an easy job, but a lifelong struggle requiring endless vigilance and rigorous self-discipline, for we are indeed giving up a part of ourselves—our egotism. If we seek to know our spiritual nature, we must be prepared to sacrifice; we must be prepared to analyze our emotional make-up and systematically eliminate all of our negative, destructive traits.

If we seek to walk the upper path, we must first pass through the doorway marked "Initiation." There is a probationary period we must go through before achieving enlightenment and being led into the full illumination. In every school of learning, a student must pass the necessary entrance requirements before being accepted. It is the same with the higher consciousness. This learning cannot be forced; it evolves through a person by a natural process as one evolves his or her own consciousness through studying, meditating, and living the life.

But once we make the conscious decision to align ourselves with the spiritual world, persistently endeavoring to overcome our lower nature, we seem to receive help from some Unseen Force. That, at least, is what all the great teachers have told us; and we can feel safe in believing that help will come to us through one avenue or another. We are never alone in our battle if we are willing to turn to Spirit Within for assistance. If we persist in our determination, in our singlemindedness, insight and strength will come to us in various ways and from various sources. Here, too, knowledge of the path ahead is invaluable, as well as the cultivation of the love of wisdom. In a sublime sense, when we study the works of great thinkers who have crossed the threshold before us, our insight is awakened through appreciating theirs; and we may discover inner realms which they explored long ago. Dr. Fleet writes that "when a person reaches a certain stage of spiritual consciousness, there comes a time when he is able to see without eyes, and to hear without ears. This individual is in touch with another world, one that is more real than this physical world. One becomes truly conscious of his Divinity and his immortality, and that is precisely the condition that all mankind years for, even though they may not be conscious of it."

There are many aspirants for the spiritual plane of life, but not many are able to attain it. As recorded in Scripture: "Many are called, but few are chosen.'' This simply means that very few people have the necessary determination to keep on with the struggle until they discover the light on the path. Usually an aspirant for the higher consciousness has been brought to it by suffering much from the superficialities of the world. She has experienced much that life has to offer and has become weary and satiated. Suffering makes her long for a higher life, and her inner cry is heard echoing throughout the universe. She is led here and there to the knowledge that will enable her to find the higher path. Now a candidate for the more advanced spiritual expression, as she earnestly attempts to achieve self-mastery, she begins to attract assistance to herself. Through the medium of the laws of resonance and vibration, she draws kindred souls, from this plane and others, who enrich her mentally and spiritually.

This type of person is attaining to great wisdom. He knows intuitively that clinging to the lower self will mean that the path will be beset with difficulties and repeated pains, sorrows, and disappointments. At times, while fighting the inner battle, he secures brief glimpses of the beauty of the spiritual realm, and knows that it is the One Reality. The spiritual realm is one of inward harmony, or perfect justice, of eternal love. As time goes on, he begins to recognize the Oneness of all life and realizes that he can no longer harm others because all life is One; therefore, hurting another means harming oneself. Simultaneously, this person recognizes that helping another also means helping oneself, and the truth of ''it is more blessed to give than to receive'' becomes a reality in his or her life.

As you overcome your lower self, as you overcome the things which people love most and cling to with such fierce tenacity, the ego and physical pleasures, you will have left behind all confusion. You will enter into a profoundly beautiful simplicity, one which may be frowned upon as foolish by the worldly-wise who are enmeshed in their network of error. You will have realized the highest wisdom, and you will be at peace. Having entered the region of reality, you will accomplish everything without striving, and all problems will easily be faced and handled by you. You will concern yourself not with changing events, but with the unchanging *principle* behind all things. Having yielded up your negativity, your egotism, your will to power, your biases and prejudices, you will enter into possession of the knowledge of higher worlds. As you surrender all without reservation, you will gain all; and you will find ''the peace that passeth all understanding.

There are four levels of imaging: the physical, mental, emotional, and spiritual. We live on all four planes and must take care of every aspect of our being. An all-embracing affirmation which I particularly

153

like is: "I am becoming aware of my oneness with the Infinite." This fulfills the law which Christ expressed as "seek ye first the Kingdom of Heaven, and all else will be added unto you." You might try saying this affirmation as you fall asleep each night; you'll be surprised at the difference it will make in your life!

Affirmations such as this can help us achieve, in our long progress of evolution, the sixth phase of creation, cosmic consciousness. Eventually, some day, in another dimension of awareness, we shall achieve the final destiny of the evolution of consciousness: complete unity of Spirit with Itself, the merging of our self-consciousness back into the One, but now with greater understanding, greater awareness, and enlightenment.

Dr. Fleet states:

> *Only when we have ceased to rely on our perishable, physical self, and learned to trust in boundless measure the Creative Power, are we prepared for unity with the One. Then for us there will be no more regret, nor disappointment, nor loneliness, nor remorse; for where all selfishness has ceased, these sufferings cannot be. When we realize the profound simplicity of spiritual consciousness, and have an unbiased, tranquil, blessed state of mind, we will know that whatever happens to us is for our own good. We will be content, and no longer the servant of the self, but the servant of the Divine. We will have nothing to defend, nothing to conceal, nothing to attack, and no interests to guard; therefore, we will be at peace.*
>
> *To become one with the Infinite is the goal of man, and is a far greater possession than anything else the world has to offer. The man or woman who attains it will know the secret of immortality.*

**FINIS**

# APPENDIX A

## RELAXATION CONCEPT

Make yourself perfectly comfortable in every way. Be sure the room is quiet and you will not be distracted. Turn down the lights.

Now you are going to relax, thoroughly relax, from head to toe. Starting with your breathing, take three deep breaths, very slowly, and with every breath you will go deeper into a state of profound relaxation.

Now your breathing is returning to normal, but with every breath you take you are relaxing even further. You are now breathing in a calm, regulated manner, and you are forgetting the cares of this day, thinking of nothing but your own bodily process of relaxation, and allowing yourself to drift down even deeper.

Now, starting with the head area, all the muscles in that area are beginning to relax. Around the skull, the forehead, deep within the head area, complete relaxation of those muscles is now taking place, so that there is no tension whatsoever in this area. Now this relaxed feeling is going into your eyes, your eyelids, and deep within your eyes, relaxing all the tiny muscles in and around and behind your eyes; letting your eyelids just feel loose and limp, and relaxed. No tension whatsoever.

The relaxation is travelling down your face now, to the muscles of your cheeks, your mouth, tongue, and on down to your jaw, relaxing all of the muscles of the chin. Just letting go of all tension and enjoying this deep, calm relaxation. This wonderful relaxed feeling is now going into your neck, around the throat, to the back of your neck, so that your entire head area is now completely relaxed.

This relaxed feeling is now going into your shoulders, releasing their tension; just letting go, letting go completely, relaxing every muscle in this part of your body, and travelling down your arms, to your hands and fingers. Now your shoulders are feeling loose and limp and relaxed, and a warm but pleasant heaviness descends down your body as you rest here in perfect relaxation, thinking of nothing but the peace of the moment.

And now your chest area is responding to this feeling of

restfulness, so that all tension in that area is completely released. Your breathing is perfectly relaxed and regular, and there is complete relaxation in your upper torso. You are now relaxing your stomach muscles—more and more—so that with every breath you take you will allow yourself to drift down even deeper.

This relaxed sensation is now travelling down your back, down that wonderfully intricate spinal cord that connects all of the nerves of your body, and branching out from it to the entire nervous system, relaxing all of your nerves. Going deeper and deeper into this wonderful state of relaxation, because it feels so good to be just letting go like this and giving all of your muscles and nerves a chance to rejuvenate themselves.

And now all the muscles and organs in the lower part of your body are relaxing. The bladder, kidneys, and organs connected with your elminative system are completely relaxed. You do not need to picture these, just give the order to the Consciousness within: relax now. There will be no muscle too tight and none too loose; every muscle will have perfect tone.

This relaxed feeling is now descending into your lower back, the pelvic region, and going down into your legs, relaxing each muscle more and more. And it feels so good to be so completely relaxed. You can feel this deep relaxation in the powerful muscles of the buttocks, travelling down your thighs, legs, knees, calves, ankles, and on down to the bottom of your feet, so that now you are completely encompassed by a wonderful, warm feeling of deep peace and relaxation.

A feeling of serenity, of peace and tranquility is now covering your entire body, and you are responding to it, because it feels so good to be so completely relaxed like this. You feel completely calm, completely at peace. More relaxed than you have been in a long time. All the tensions of the past week have left your body, and while you are in this relaxed state, your body is in a position to begin adjusting itself and express in a more healthy way. We know that when we are completely relaxed like this we can then begin directing the Innate Power to make any adjustments that are necessary in order to bring your body to a more healthy expression, and It is doing so now.

Continue to rest here for a few moments while Spirit Within brings your body to a state of perfectly normal functioning.

# APPENDIX B

## Suggestions For Self-Hypnosis

The following is a sample induction talk, which you can use as is, or adapt to your own personality style. If you wish, you can tape record this talk as an aid in learning self-hypnosis. You could record your own voice, or have someone with a soft, pleasant voice record it for you.

Now that you are completely comfortable with your eyes closed, just listen to the sound of my voice, which will help to relax you even further, and follow all the suggestions given.

I want you to imagine that you are going into the lobby of a large hotel, and walking up to the elevators. Press the button marked "down." In a moment when your elevator arrives, this will be your own private elevator, perfectly safe in every way, that's going to help carry you down closer to the depths of your subconscious mind.

Now the elevator is arriving, the doors are opening, and you step inside. As you look upward above the doors, you will see a panel of buttons marked from 1 to 10, and the light is now on at the button marked 1. In a moment at my count, your elevator will begin descending, going all the way down to the tenth floor. When you arrive at the tenth floor, you will get off into a room that has a big, soft, comfortable bed, that you can go over to, and lie down, and have a wonderful rest.

1. Relaxation is settling over your forehead and eyelids.

2. Relax your shoulder and neck muscles.

3. Relaxing the muscles in your arms and hands. Deeper and deeper with each breath. The more thoroughly that you can relax, the deeper you will be able to go into hypnosis.

4. Now you are relaxing the muscles in your entire back, all the way down your shoulders; limp and relaxed. You are so relaxed and so comfortable.

5. You are beginning to drift deeper and deeper as you relax the muscles of your abdomen and let go. Let go still more. Notice your breathing. You are now breathing slowly and deeply, and with every breath you take you allow yourself to drift even deeper into self-hypnosis.

6. Now you are relaxing your hips, thighs and buttocks, and this wonderful relaxed feeling is travelling down your legs. Every muscle, nerve and fibre of your body is now completely, deeply relaxed.

7. You are drifting down more rapidly now, and going even deeper.

8. Now your legs and feet are completely relaxed, and you are in a state of deep relaxation from the top of your head to the tips of your toes.

9. Now you have released all the tension from your entire body, and these tensions will not disturb you again. More and more relaxed.

10. Now your elevator has arrived, and the doors are opening, and you step into this room and see this big, soft, comfortable bed, all made up for you. And you can just go right over there and stretch out on that bed, and go now into a very pleasant hypnotic sleep.

Total relaxation is now over your entire body. Your mind is completely at ease. Your mind is very quiet. You are now in a very pleasant, deep hypnotic sleep. And your subconscious mind is very aware of what I am saying and wants to obey all of my instructions, because you consciously desire to do so.

While you are in hypnosis if any emergency should arise, you will immediately return to your normal, waking state, and be wide awake and fully alert.

Whenever you are ready to awaken all you need to do is count from 1 to 5 and, at the count of 5, you will return to your normal, outer consciousness, feeling completely refreshed and rejuvenated in every way.

If you do not succeed in achieving total relaxation, use another method to deepen the relaxation, such as imagining yourself walking through the woods, and lying down on the soft, green grass, and relaxing even further.

Here are some sample suggestions that can be used for particular problems:

## WEIGHT LOSS

From now on you are going to eat smaller meals. When you eat your regular meals each day, each meal will consist of much less food than you have been eating in the past. Your appetite is decreasing. Your appetite is now decreasing, and you are going to want much less food than you normally eat. It will be very easy for you to do this. You find that you simply do not require as much food as you have been eating, and you will not go hungry. You will be perfectly satisfied with smaller quantities of food, and you will not feel deprived of food in any way.

From now on you are going to stick to your diet rigidly, and you will enjoy it. You are going to have all the will power and self-discipline you need to stick to this diet, and it will not be a sacrifice. You will enjoy doing it, as you watch the pounds melt away every day.

From now on you will eat smaller, nutritionally beneficial, non-fattening meals, and you will have absolutely no desire to eat between meals. You will be able to go longer from one mealtime to another, and you will not have the need to have any snacks. When you finish your dinner you will have absolutely no desire for second helpings or for desert, and you will easily be able to go until the next mealtime without eating anything else.

Fattening foods no longer appeal to you. In fact, the thought of eating them is repellent to you. You will no longer desire to eat fattening foods such as ice-cream, candy, cakes and pie. (Or whatever your particular favorite is).

At this point begin visualizing yourself stepping on the scale and seeing your desired weight. See yourself wearing clothes you could not get into before, and see others telling you how nice you look. (Take at least three minutes to do this).

You are not going to allow anything to prevent you from reaching your desired goal of —— pounds. And your subconscious mind is now helping you to achieve this goal, and when you reach it, you will easily be able to maintain it. This is coming true for you now.

## STOPPING SMOKING

Your subconscious mind is now completely and totally erasing the habit of smoking from its records. It has erased all the reasons and causes for your smoking. From now on you have absolutely no reason to smoke, you do not enjoy smoking. So I want you to say to yourself mentally now: "This is the end of my smoking habit. I am now a non-smoker." As you say this, you feel very pleased about it. You are very happy that you no longer need this crutch in your life. Your habit of smoking has been entirely and completely eliminated from your life. It is completely erased from the records of your subconscious mind, which now recognizes you as a non-smoker. You do not need to smoke, you do not want to smoke, and you do not like to smoke. You have no desire, craving, or temptation to smoke, and you will never have a desire, craving or temptation to smoke ever again. Smoking does not exist in your life. You will always think of yourself as a non-smoker.

(At this point visualize yourself in various scenes in which you habitually smoked in the past. See yourself in these situations as a non-smoker, feeling calm and relaxed.)

You will never feel any nervousness or irritability or any other side effects or withdrawal symptoms as a result of stopping smoking. You will not feel any discomfort from this, instead you will feel totally healthy and energetic. You will not replace the habit of smoking with eating, or any other undesirable habit. You are now a non-smoker. Your subconscious mind now sees and accepts you as a non-smoker. Smoking no longer exists in your life, and you feel very pleased about this.

## SELF-CONFIDENCE

Your subconscious mind is now erasing any memory of ever having been programmed to the idea of not having sufficient confidence. Your subconscious mind is now accepting the image of your total self-confidence. From this moment on you will have no difficulty in accomplishing whatever you wish to accomplish. You have all the confidence you need to handle your life successfully. Your confidence is increasing daily. You will have no

159

difficulty whatsoever in being completely confident in every situation. You are seeing yourself this way now.

At this point begin visualizing yourself in situations in which formerly you had lacked sufficient confidence. See yourself smiling, happy and confident, totally self-assured.

As each day passes you are gaining more confidence in yourself as a person of worth and value, and you are developing a true inner strength which will be of great help to you as you go about your daily life.

You now have a new confident image of yourself as a person of worth and value, and all of your activities will be carried out with perfect confidence, easily and effortlessly. You are now in touch with your true inner self-confidence, and you will be able to express this outwardly.

Classes in the PSYCHOLOGY OF SUCCESSFUL LIVING
are conducted regularly in the San Francisco Bay Area
by Dr. Hiatt. Contact her at:
P.O. Box 28814,
San Jose, Ca 95159
or Telephone: (408) 287-5180

Classes in CONCEPT-THERAPY are conducted regularly
throughout the United States and Canada by the
Concept-Therapy Institute
25550 Boerne Stage Road,
San Antonio, Texas 78228.
(Please send for free brochures)

# BIBLIOGRAPHY AND RECOMMENDED BOOKS

Adar, Robert, (Ed.), **Psychoneuroimmunology**, Academic Press, New York, 1982.

Allen, James, **As a Man Thinketh**, Collins Publishers, London.

Assagioli, Roberto, **Psychosynthesis**, Hobbs, Dorman & Co., New York, 1965.

Badgley, Laurence E., **Healing AIDS Naturally**, Human Energy Press, 1987.

Bailey, Herbert, **Vitamin E, Your Key to a Healthy Heart**, ARC Books, Inc., New York, 1969.

Benson, Herbert, with M.Z. Klipper, **The Relaxation Response**, William Morrow, New York, 1975.

Bolton, Brett, **The Secret Power of Plants**, Berkeley Medallion Books, New York, 1974.

Boone, J. Allen, **Kinship With All Life**, Harper & Row, New York, 1954.

**Brain/Mind Bulletin**, P.O. Box 42211, Los Angeles, Ca 90042

Bricklin, Mark, **Rodale's Encyclopedia of National Home Remedies**, Rodale Press, Emmaus, Pa 1982.

Bry, Adelaide, **Directing the Movies of Your Mind**, Harper & Row, 1978.

Bucke, Dr. Maurice, **Cosmic Consciousness**, E.P. Dutton & Co., New York, 1901.

Capra, Fritjof, **The Tao of Physics**, Bantam, 1974.

Clark, Linda, **Know Your Nutrition**, Keats Pub. Co., New Cannan, Conn., 1973.

Cousins, Norman, **The Healing Heart,** Norton Books, New York, 1983.

Davis, Roy Eugene, **Creative Imagination**, Davis Enterprises, Garret Park, Md., 1961.

DeChardin, Teilhard, **The Phenomena of Man**, POM Project, 8600 Casabana Ave., Canoga Park, Ca.

Emery, Stewart, **Actualizations**, Dolphin Books, 1978.

Fleet, Dr. Thurman, **Rays of the Dawn**, Concept-Therapy Institute, Route 8, Box 250, San Antonio, Texas, 78228. Hardbound: $5, no tax.

Fox, Arnold, M.D., **The Beverly Hills Diet**, Bantam Books, 1981.

Gawain, Shakti, **Creative Visualization**, Whatever Publications, Berkeley, Ca, 1979.

Gillies, Jerry, **Money-Love**, Warner Books, 1978.

Hardison, James, **Let's Touch**, Prentice-Hall, 1980.

Hill, Napoleon, **Think and Grow Rich**, Fawcett Books, 1970.

Hudson, Thomas Jay, **The Law of Psychic Phenomena**, Hudson-Cohan Publishing Co., 1970.

Hutschnecker, Arnold, **The Will to Live**, Pocket Books, Inc., New York, 1961.

Huxley, Laura, **You Are Not the Target**, Farrar, Straus & Co., New York, 1963.

Justice, Blair, **Who Gets Sick: Thinking and Health**, Peale Press, Houston, Texas, 77019.

Keyes, Ken, Jr., **Handbook to Higher Consciousness**, Ken Keyes Center, Coos Bay, OR, 1974.

LeCron, Leslie M., **Self-Hypnotism**, Signet Books, 1964.

LeShan, Lawrence, **You Can Fight For Your Life**, Evans & Co., New York, 1977.

Maslow, A., **The Farther Reaches of Human Nature,,** Viking, New York, 1971.

Mason, L. John.,**A Guide to Stress Reduction**, Celestial Arts, Millbrae, Ca

Mendelsohn, R.S., **Confessions of a Medical Heretic**, Warner Books, New York, 1979.

Moody, Patrick, **The Supernutrition Handbook,** Stanton Press, 235 Gough St., San Francisco, 94102

Neil, A., **Health and Healing,** Houghton Mifflin, Boston, 1983.

Ornstein, Robert, and David Sobel, **The Healing Brain,** Simon & Shuster, New York, 1987.

Oyle, Dr. Irving, **The Healing Mind,** Celestial Arts, Millbrae, Ca., 1974.

Padus, Emrika, and the Editors of PREVENTION Magazine, **The Complete Guide to Your Emotions and Your Health,** Rodale Press, Emmaus, Pa., 1986.

Passwater, Richard A., **Supernutrition,** Pocket Books, New York, 1975.

Pearce, Dr. Joseph, **The Crack in the Cosmic Egg,** Pocket Books, New York.

Pearson, Durk, and Sandy Shaw, **Life Extension,** Warner Books, 1982.

Peck, Scott, **The Road Less Travelled,** Walker & Co., 1985.

Pelletier, Dr. K., **Mind as Healer, Mind as Slayer,** Dell Pub. Co., New York, 1977.

Ray, Sondra, **I Deserve Love,** Les Femmes Pub., Millbrae, Ca. 1976.

Reuben, C., and J. Priestley, **Essential Supplements for Women,** Putnam & Sons, 1989.

Rodale, J.I., **Happy People Rarely Get Cancer,** Rodale Press, Emmaus, Pa 1970.

Rodin, J., **Coping and Health,** Plenum Books, New York, 1979.

Selye, Hans, M.D., **The Stress of Life,** McGraw Hill, New York, 1976.

Siegal, Bernie, **Love, Medicine and Miracles,** Harper & Row, New York, 1986.

Simeons, A.T.W., **Man's Presumptuous Brain,** E.P. Dutton & Co., New York, 1962.

Simone, C.B., **Cancer and Nutrition,** McGraw-Hill, New York, 1983.

Simonton, Dr. C., et al., **Getting Well Again,** Tarcher, New York, 1978.

Wright, Jonathan, M.D., **Dr. Wright's Book of Nutritional Therapy,** Rodale Press, Emmaus, Pa., 1979.

Zilbergeld, Bernie, and Arnold Lazarus, **Mind Power Through Mental Training,** Little Brown & Co., 1987.